African American Pamphlet Collection

The Nutshell

The System of American Slavery

African American Pamphlet Collection

The Nutshell
The System of American Slavery

ISBN/EAN: 9783743314191

Manufactured in Europe, USA, Canada, Australia, Japa

Cover: Foto ©ninafisch / pixelio.de

Manufactured and distributed by brebook publishing software
(www.brebook.com)

African American Pamphlet Collection

The Nutshell

PRICE 25 CENTS SINGLE; $2 PER DOZEN; $10 PER HUNDRED

THE NUTSHELL.

THE SYSTEM OF AMERICAN SLAVERY
"TESTED BY SCRIPTURE,"

BEING

"A SHORT METHOD" WITH PRO-SLAVERY D.D's, WHETHER
DOCTORS OF DIVINITY, OR OF DEMOCRACY,

EMBRACING AXIOMS OF

SOCIAL, CIVIL, AND POLITICAL ECONOMY,
AS DIVINELY IMPRESSED UPON THE HUMAN
CONSCIENCE AND SET FORTH IN DIVINE REVELATION.

IN TWO LECTURES.

BY A LAYMAN OF THE PROTESTANT EPISCOPAL CHURCH IN THE DIOCESE
OF CONNECTICUT.

TO WHICH ARE ADDED BRIEF EXTRACTS, "TEACHINGS OF
PATRIOTS AND STATESMEN," &c., &c.

ALSO,

An Outline Compend of the African Slave-Trade.

NEW YORK:
PUBLISHED FOR THE AUTHOR.
1862.

ADVERTISEMENT.

On submitting the following Lectures to the public through the press, it is to be noted, a full year has elapsed since their preparation. No essential modification seems dictated by the intervening changing scenes of the drama of Rebellion, however these may present many important suggestions, as experience ever does, illustrative of the fundamental and unchangeable truths here laid down; so with little or no variation from their original draft, nor yet leaving the experience of the year unimproved, as may be suggested in the sequel, we submit these Lectures to the enlightened conscience and judgment of the *true* philanthropic and patriotic American Unionist.

A word as to our title-page. A "NUTSHELL" is presumed to be closely filled with nutricious meat, in all its compartments. Ours is easily cracked, but cannot be rifled. *Warranted good for long years.*

As these Lectures, not originally prepared for the specific purpose of being published, have been, in manuscript, decidedly approved by most competent judges, as well adapted to be extensively and permanently useful: no affectation of diffidence shall belie the implied concurrence of the Author, by their publication. The *principal* motive is: that after three score years of her "nursing case and protection," to do our "Country some service," in perhaps the most practicable mode; (since unused to fight, yet not to write;) and thus contribute to *unity of counsel,* tending at least to *unity of policy,* toward the only sure overthrow of Rebellion. Only "Righteousness exalteth a nation, but sin is a reproach to any people."

It is specially designed that in all places where the "Nutshell" (*warranted full of nutricious meat*) may be sold in considerable quantities, as on occasions of the public delivery of these Lectures; all surplus profits thence arising, exceeding fair remuneration, shall be appropriated to any fund for the relief of sick and wounded soldiers or sailors, or similar object.

April, 1862.

PREFACE.

A FEW pages of the Lectures here presented were outlined soon after the National Fast of 4th of January last, with special reference to certain sermons, addresses, &c., which had recently appeared in apology, defence or justification of the "Institution" of American slavery. That outline served but to familiarize the subject, and more clearly to indicate the proper field of argument, as based upon the concurrence of the innate, unsophisticated *Human Conscience* with the Holy Scriptures, applying to these the Key of our Blessed Saviour—"*But in the beginning it was not so.*"

With this incipient preparation, the present Lectures are the result of the almost impromptu operations of the mind of the writer, with the open Bible, as the pen progressed. However these same reasonings may have been presented by others, neither the plan nor mode of presenting or applying them have been borrowed, for in the way of reading, the writer had given the subject but a very limited and cursory attention; while coincidences will be both rational and corroborative. The *plan,* as appears, was not prescribed. but evolved in execution. It is not to be overlooked, as a pre-requisite and legitimate preparation for the argument, the fundamental position assigned to the HUMAN CONSCIENCE.

The termerity of an humble layman, in attempting a refutation of the subtle sophistries of learned Doctors in Divinity and Law, is not without precedent, as the encounter with a sling and a stone, against shield and spear, is an ever memorable example; and we *hope,* without arrogance, in the present case, with like result. We say—with like result—yet herewith concurring,

> " The man convinced against his will,
> Is of the same opinion still;"
> So too Goliath slain, must fill
> His fitting place—Goliath still.
>
> Or,   So too, indeed, Goliath slain,
> His fitting place must needs retain.

June, 1861.

INTRODUCTION.

"AND Elihu said, Great men are not always wise.
But there is a spirit in man, and the Inspiration of the
Almighty giveth them understanding. Therefore I
also will show mine opinion." "For the spirit within
me constraineth me." See Job XXXII entire.

In the great "Conflict of Ages,"—of the supremacy
of Good over Evil—of Truth over Error—the proposition is incontrovertible, that the simple moral elements, Goodness and Truth, command the ready concurrence of the heaven-derived HUMAN CONSCIENCE.
Yet is it a remarkable and lamentable fact, so-great
diversity exists as to the particular combinations and
phases through which these elements become tangi-
ble, visible, and operative, in the field of actual "conflict." It would surely be passing strange,—but that
herein is the "conflict,"—that where all are equally
interested in preserving the genuine currency of
Heaven's mint, counterfeit coin of evil should become
any considerable proportion of the circulation,—more
strange that it should supplant the genuine, and yet
more—that the counterfeiters themselves should boldly advocate, even with immunity, the equality—aye,
superiority of the bogus coin. The question as to "the
baptism of John, was it of Heaven, or of men?" (or,
H—ll), would be equally pertinent, as to Freedom, or
Slavery.

And yet it has come to pass, *Mirabile Dictu!* when
grave and reverend Doctors of Divinity, not only find
apology for Slavery, as a *Providential evil* in the world,
eschewing its inherent sinfulness, but boldly assert its
Divine institution, as displaying in eminent degree the
Divine Love and Benevolence. And we are not a little pained to mark the assent of some whom we most

highly esteem, love and venerate, for their work's
sake : that Slavery is not, *per se*, sin, or in any proper
sense, of original Evil.

Although ever disposed to a lenient judgment on
the system of Slavery, as of other evils consequent to
a state of Probation, which Earth, since the fall, ever
has been, is, and until the Millennium,will be ; and, but
for the present wicked rebellion, unparalleled since
that of the rebel angels, we would have volunteered
an apology for the *"peculiar institution,"* as not absolutely irreconcileable, under "peculiar" circumstances, with Christian profession : we were not, however,
prepared to hear its absolution, nay, *justification*, on
principles of Christianity, but were impelled by the
"Spirit in man" to reconsider the whole matter, and
"Search the Scriptures to see if these things were
so." The result of this examination, intent for truth,
for truth's sake, is somewhat analagous to the case of
an Ancient Seer, when called to curse Israel, reversing
the predicates as to the System of American slavery.
In the former case, blessing, instead of cursing ; in the
latter, condemnation, instead of palliation. Hence the
following

LECTURES :
BIBLICAL, MORAL, AND POLITICAL.

We first propose for our strict observance in the
progress of this examination, these following implied
cautions :—"Not handling the word of God deceitfully, but by manifestation of the truth, commending ourselves to every man's conscience in the sight of God."
2d Cor. IV : 2.

" Wo unto them that call evil good, and good evil ;
that put darkness for light, and light for darkness ;
that put bitter for sweet, and sweet for bitter." Isa.
v : 20.

But for the grand test of Truth in religious and
moral teaching, concurrent with the innate "Con-

science,"—"spirit in man,"—"inspiration of the Almighty," shall be the rule of our Blessed Saviour.

"IN THE BEGINNING IT WAS NOT SO."

O the glorious simplicity and comprehensiveness of Divine Truth! Here indeed, as in a nutshell, is embraced the entire argument. The conclusion is at once apparent, inevitable, irresistable. Polemics have no place. The soul, telegraphed from Heaven, through its own unrivalled Electric-Thought, with a derisive compassion, dispenses with the plodding logic of hoof, or engine ; of induction, or syllogism ; already rejoicing in the *truth,* and "inwardly digesting" the precept "Whatsoever ye would that men should do unto you do ye even so unto them."

While buckling on our armor, the victory is won. The walls of Modern Jericho—citadel of Slavery— have fallen, ere the ram's-horns have sounded. Let it then be our pleasure, and our invigorating exercise, since spared the labor, to note the stations more prominent, past which we have sped. Nor in our progress do we care to please the *hyper-critical.*

In laying the foundation of our argument we but follow a truly illustrious example—declaring—"*We hold these truths to be self-evident,*" &c. Thus we premise—It is an incontrovertible Truth : There is a moral, mutual relation of man to man, underlying all possible accidental conditions of his being, established by his Creator, as a fundamental law of his existence, involving common necessities, with common mutual duty and dependence. To vary the proposition,—Man is eminently a *Moral Agent*—and no voluntary act of his can be dissevered from the moral obligation of love and obedience to God, and what "is like unto it" —equal, reciprocal good will to his fellow-man. Hence it is not only eminently fit and proper—"*meet and right, but our bounden duty at all times, and in all places,*" yea under all possible circumstances, in every voluntary act, first of all, to settle the question of its *moral* character.

It is also self-evident, superceding proof, that the innate *Human Conscience,* unsophisticated, "unseared," is the proper faculty in man for apprehending *moral* truth and duty. The intellectual powers are its counsellers, while itself approves, or condemns.

Be it freely admitted that the Bible, as the basis of Protestant Christianity, God's revelation to man, is the proper rule of faith and practice ; yet it is not so much an *original* revelation, as a rescript, a reminder, of the Divine law written upon the heart. True, " All Scripture is given by inspiration of God, and is profitable for doctrine, for reproof, for correction, for instruction in righteousness." " But there is a spirit in man, and the Inspiration of the Almighty giveth them understanding." This " Inspiration of the Almighty" is "that Light which lighteth every man that cometh into the world"—the Divinely inspired *Human Conscience.* Hereby was " God's own image " so impressed on man, that he thence " became a living soul." A mystery this, we remark incidentally, akin to the miraculous incarnation of our Blessed Saviour. Conscience is truly and spiritually " God with us." It is the more special and essential medium or mode of God's omnipresence to every child of Adam, however surrounded by his Providence. It is that faculty of the soul which seeks and reciprocates truth in the love of it. Hence with peculiar force is the appeal of the great Apostle—" Commending ourselves to *every man's conscience* in the sight of God." It is important to note, the conscience of *every man* must be essentially the *same,* since the same appeal is to " *every man's conscience.*" God's " Image," as Himself, is unchangeable, the same, yesterday, to-day, and forever ; the same in all men ; in all ages.

Our purpose is to establish clearly the entire concurrence of conscience with Divine revelation, in defining man's particular duties and relations, and that too with special reference to Slavery. We therefore will endeavor to cultivate the most intimate acquaintance with this Divine representative, although *"he be not far from every one of us."*

The mandates of a wise and good King are commended less by his power, than to the love and loy-

8

alty—the *conscience*, of his subjects. So God's written word or revelation is ever addressed to an approving conscience, we mean, conscience *unseared.* Conscience is the inward Monitor of the soul—the intuitive discerner between right and wrong; with unerring precision approving or condemning, to the full measure of moral responsibility. It may indeed be silenced by the imperious usurpations of a perverse will. It suspends judgment while the passions rule, but becomes a fierce accuser, " biting like a serpent and stinging like an adder, until a *genuine* repentance, insuring free forgiveness.

Every sin is arraigned at the bar of conscience, although the God-given and true, may for the time be ejected from the judgment seat, or supplanted by a false, an artificial, a mock conscience, quieting itself in the perversion, or deceitful handling, of God's word. He is a bold sinner in defiance of conscience, but will rather substitute its semblance. And yet as we fear, there *is* a fathomless depth, without even its semblance, from which no appeal to Conscience meets response. To any one so irrecoverably lost, we address no argument. " Cast not your pearls before swine."

Of the true, Divinely inspired Conscience, has an eminent saint (Bp. Wilson) exclaimed—"Better die a thousand deaths, than sin against my Conscience."

So also the poet—

> " What conscience dictates to be done,
> Or warns me not to do,
> This, teach me more than hell to shun,
> That, more than heaven pursue."

It is often argued, that those best acquainted with certain conditions of life, are best qualified to judge of their moral character ; and therefore the truest judgment of Slavery, is to be found in slave communities. As well may we look for an enlightened and true judgment on the subject of Intemperance, in grog shops; on chastity and moral purity, in brothels; on fraud and theft, among knaves and thieves; on treason, among traitors; on sins of any sort, among the habitually sinning.

Implication in sin is a key to its apology, or justification. It may be safely assumed, had Slavery never existed in our nation, not a single Doctor of Divinity of our ten thousand clergy could be found, who would stake his orthodoxy on a Bible defence of the institution. It may also be safely assumed, no national sin could withstand the united efforts of a faithful Gospel Ministry in a Christian nation. Will not they be held justly responsible for the sins which they palliate or justify, whose special office and duty it is, to " cry aloud and spare not, and show the people their transgressions " ?

It is a very adroit exculpation, to charge the sin upon its occasion ; most satisfactory indeed as to the sin of Slavery, it having long, long ago, been saddled upon our nation—yes, *Providentially !* This was precisely the method of our first parents. Eve charged her sin upon the Serpent who beguiled her ; and Adam, almost directly upon God himself. " The woman whom *thou gavest* to be with me, she gave me of the tree and I did eat."

Still will the apologist of Slavery reiterate, as, though hard pressed on the open field of argument, seeking shelter in this strong-hold, deemed impregnable—"Surely, it exists by God's Providence." And what, indeed, in the Material or Moral Universe, does not exist by God's Providence—ordained, commanded, or permitted ? Joseph sold by his brethren, " *who meant it for evil ;* " the Saviour, " *by wicked hands crucified and slain ;* " yea, Hell itself ! into which " the wicked shall be turned, and all the nations that forget God." To plead God's Providence in palliation of sin, is but impious audacity. The *occasions* of sin are but the incidents of a state of probation, necessary as such, yet not necessitating the sin ; but are equal occasions of Virtue and Godliness, in shunning or resisting temptation.

Conscience—for we cannot become too familiar with this inward monitor, the moral light of the soul,—is in its nature inextinguishable ; however it may be temporarily smothered. It is the Porter at the gate:

the watchman of the heart's citadel; charged with double duty, first as monitor, second, as accuser and witness. Drugged by an opiate, or felled by a blow; it may fail in the first; but will surely recover to perform its final duty of accuser and witness.

Reason and Conscience, though not identical, are inseparable companions. Both concur in truth and duty. As there are Axioms in Philosophy, self-evident truths, which the intellect without effort intuitively accepts; so there are Axioms in Morals as readily accepted by Conscience, and alike adopted by Reason. That Good, and Evil, are essentially distinct, antagonistic principles, involving weal, or woe, is a Moral Axiom, as self-evident to the Conscience, as that a whole equals all its parts, is self-evident to the Intellect. Both propositions alike supersede proof. Nor can the essentially Evil, be made essentially Good, or *vice versa.* " Wo to them that call evil good, and good evil."

It is evident that for wise purposes, inscrutable by us, yet apprehensible, as suited to a state of moral probation, these antagonistic elements, Good and Evil, have ever been the conflicting attendants upon our common humanity, consequent upon "the taste of that forbidden tree, which brought death into the world, and all our woe." From these elements are derived the only *moral* qualities which pertain to human acts.

"Do men gather grapes of thorns, or figs of thistles?" Is it wise to cultivate thorns and thistles, or will not the good husbandman rather eradicate the noxious growth? What if an enemy hath sown tares among the wheat; however prudently he may await the harvest, lest in eradicating the tares he root up the wheat also; will he not the more carefully exclude foul seed from adjoining fields?

The existence of Evil, is a problem not here to be discussed; the individual sin is in preferring, adopting it. "It must needs be that offences will come; but woe to him by whom the offence cometh." It must needs be that evil exist in a state of probation; but woe to him who calls it Good. Until the Millennium, Evil may never be sensibly diminished, but rather may culminate as now it would seem, Satan loosed, the Hydra of the infernal lake, defying vastly greater than Herculean strength ; Slavery being chief of its hundred heads. Since Evil is permitted in this state of probation ; and, since laws may not eradicate, they are necessarily enacted to regulate and restrain ; shall we therefore justify it, "call evil good" ?

With the light of a *truthful* conscience thus trimmed and burning, we will be also none the less aided by that corresponding light, the word of God. "Thy word is a lamp unto my feet, and a light unto my path." These tests are to each other, *mutual ;* and on all moral questions, *concurrent.* With these answering Lights, we will proceed now to examine both the Christianity, and Morality, of the *System of American Slavery;* utterly destitute, as we shall find, of a redeeming feature, as to its *legal status ;* albeit a few scattered rays from the sun of Christianity may penetrate the interstices of its prison walls ; and the sympathies of a genial humanity may in greater or less degree lighten the oppression of its chains. We condemn not the gradation of allotments by which, Providentially, very many are called to subordinate duties ;—a moderate servitude even, if it be not robbery of one's self, or of God, rendering an equivalent, "just and equal." Such was the Jewish servitude, which for precedent, a Jewish Rabbi, with certain Christian Doctors, has presumed to denominate *Slavery !* yet its extreme was no parallel to American Slavery, as we shall see hereafter.

Leaving the Jewish Rabbi to the incidental discomfiture of his argument, as will appear from his own Scriptures, let us notice the fundamental plea of certain Christian Doctors. It is this : Whereas Slavery was tolerated under the Mosaic economy, and was prevalent in the time of our Saviour, (in point of fact, we believe it did not exist in Judea, except as connected with Roman officials, nor does it appear our Saviour ever came in contact with a slave) and he gave no positive precept against it, as on other occasions, instance the law of divorce; or again in the enumeration of sundry sins and vices—as "out of the heart proceed evil thoughts, murders, adulteries, fornications, thefts, false witness, blasphemies,"—assuming the purpose of our Saviour was to complete the catalogue of sins; therefore, *it* not being thus classified, Slavery is not, *per se*, sin. Are not indeed Treason, Arson, &c, sinful? These same Doctors will on other occasions tell us, truly too, after this manner: "It does not appear to have been the design of our Saviour to set forth a *formal code* of Christian Morals; while his incidental precepts, and example of his holy life, inculcated the highest, broadest benevolence."

Is not then the word of God handled "deceitfully," when perverted by unwarrantable inferences from its general purpose of *equal justice* and *benevolence?*—a perversion as gross, (and often much more mischievous) as to assert that our Saviour has explicitly declared, a rich man cannot enter into the kingdom of Heaven; for we know a camel cannot pass through the eye of a needle. The obviously *consonant*, is ever the *true*, acceptation of Divine teaching. We are sure also it is quite legitimate on analagous, or controverted points, to adopt the rule of right reason prescribed by our Saviour himself, as in the given case of divorce; "But in the beginning it was not so." Let us suppose the subject presented to be Polygamy, abounding to excess in highest examples. Might we not expect a similar reply—"In the beginning it was not so." Shall we palliate sins "not to be named" from the example of the daughters of Lot? of Judah?—the sin of drunkenness from that of Noah? Habitual sinners of either class, it is declared, "cannot enter into the kingdom of Heaven."

Who does not revolt at the idea of consigning captives in war to a brutal soldiery in butchery or lust? And yet it is shown, by repeated record, of the Jewish scriptures; of entire communities, captives of war; only virgins were spared to live, for apportionment among the victors.* Moses was a fugitive from justice, amenable to Egyptian law for a capital offence, nurtured too in the family of her Kings. As a simple fact it was murder, and subsequently so charged upon him by one of his own nation, whereupon he sought safety in flight. This seems however to be recorded as in line of God's judicial dispensation. It is not ours to condemn. David was brought unwittingly to pass just sentence upon himself in the character doubly criminal, presented by the Prophet. Nor in those things permitted through the "hardness of their hearts"—Polygamy, Concubinage, or Slavery—were it so—are such to be imitated. "In the beginning it was not so."

"The Scriptures were written for our instruction;" and while the example of the wicked is to be abhorred, the sins of *good men* are to be equally avoided; "for that all have sinned." Carefully as we may scan the sacred volume, "Lo this only have we found, that God made man *upright*, but *they* have sought out many inventions." These "inventions"—deviations from original "uprightness," are of necessity sinful, as their source.

Let us now recur to "the Beginning" that we may find the exact *status* of man, assigned by his Creator.

"God created man in his own image, in the image of God created he him, *a* male and *a* female created he them." (Dr. Kitto supplies the article, thus precluding Polygamy)

"And God blessed them, and God said unto them, be fruitful and multiply, and replenish the Earth, and subdue it, and have dominion over the fish of the sea, and over the fowl of the air, and over every living thing that moveth upon the face of the Earth." Gen. I. 27, 28.

(See subsequent *lost* ten verses, restored on after page.)

The man had one wife; but no slaves created in God's "own image" were included in his proper "do-

* See Judges xxi chap., including also a parallel with the Sabines of Roman history. Also Num. xxxi, 18.

minion." But man, hence all men, "for God hath created of one blood all nations to dwell upon the face of
the earth," have a common "dominion" in the entire
subordinate animal and vegetable creation, devised,
endowed, invested, by the Creator himself. It is also
pertinent to remark the special, proper, distinguishing
characteristic of man, repeatedly specified in these
records of his Creation—*"likeness," "image of God."*

Do we handle the word of God "deceitfully"—or do
we "commend ourselves to every man's conscience,"
when we assert, that all *lawful* possessions and "dominion" are clearly included in these general specifica-
tions of God's own rich, free bounty to man ? and yet
not a *slave* is implied ! Far from it; for contrarywise,
man's equality of natural rights could not be more
clear by express declaration. The proposition, de-
cried by some as *"infidel"*—"that all men are created
free and equal, and are by nature endowed with certain inalienable rights," is but the proper commentary
on this most explicit ordinance of God.

Here then, in this first Chapter of Genesis—"in the
Beginning"—do we find the original charter of the
rights of man,—the universal, fundamental, Divine
law of *Property*, *"common law"* of Christendom, enun-
ciated by God himself.

It is also pertinent to remark here, though digress-
ing somewhat from our prescribed line of argument;
nor can the monstrous idea of property in man be
maintained, but by the most incongruous superadding
to the natural relation, of property, and owner.—
Property of *right*, in all things else, requires no law
of force, as to its particular owner, guarding against
its own volition and flight. "The ox knoweth his
owner and the ass his master's crib." Property common, is naturally passive in possession, without law
appertaining, or adhering, to its owner. If of the an-
imated creation, it "knows not the voice of strangers,"
but is most docile to its owner, although it may go
astray. Its only necessary recognition by law, is the
designation of its rightful owner as distinguished from
other persons; and for legal transfer, and assessment.

Indeed it has *spoken* : "Am not I thine ass ?" True, by a figure, *"riches take wings and fly away :"*—Literally, in the Slave System, *property takes legs and runs away.* The poor slave steals himself from, his owner, say $1000—more or less. Query—which is the real thief ; the professed owner in holding, or the poor slave in stealing himself? Both cannot be right. Which of these twain must repent, that he may "escape the damnation of hell" ? We "judge not," and only add—"In the Beginning it was not so," and to "the Beginning" let us now return.

We here find man's *social* condition also prescribed, embracing his immediate relative duties, as referred to by the Psalmist. "He setteth the solitary in families." The family was instituted, of which lawful marriage is the memorial and perpetuation. Also this special injunction was given as to the material Earth, *"to subdue it."* While deriving sustenance from its fruits, it was made man's correlative duty "to till the ground." Industry then is *honorable,* as among the prescribed duties of the progenitor of the race. It may well be doubted if the toil for support, or the sorrows of maternity, should be understood as enhanced or intensified, in the sentence upon man's disobedience ; but that these perpetual conditions should become ever present monitors to man, of his so fatal forfeiture of God's favor ; like as the natural phenomenon of the "bow in the heavens," was subsequently made the sign or symbol of His mercy.

Nor is it difficult to see how irreconcilable are these primeval conditions, with the system of American Slavery, so utterly incompatible with the family institution. And we submit it to the *conscience,* if the repudiation of necessary and useful industry, in field or shop ; accounting it servile and dishonorable ; but tasking—*enslaving* a fellow-man, to an eschewed, unrequited service, be not *a,* or *the,* most wicked "invention" of man, in disobedience of God's positive command ; and in evasion of His just yet merciful sentence, "in the sweat of thy brow shalt thou eat bread." (Alas too, for the prevalent folly of delighting in the mere prod-act adapted to necessity, utility, convenience, or ornament—yet ignoring the labor, the skill, and ingenuity indispensable to the production.)

Nor did Slavery find place in the Ark; although the inference is fair that it figured prominently when the "Earth had become corrupt and was filled with violence," "and all were swept away by the flood."

These first chapters of Genesis, commonly read or referred to as mere narrative, whether accepted literally, or as an allegorical medium of instruction—the realities being too vast for human conception—are verily the *Key* to the sacred volume. In these original chronicles of the Creation, God has given a *Constitution*—*Supreme Law*—inwrought also in the *heart* and *conscience* of man, wherein is the "likeness—image of God."

God himself, in the person of His Son, our Saviour, "without whom was not anything made that was made," has placed in our hands this *Key* of the Scriptures, by example demonstrating its admirable simplicity, and adaptation to use, in unlocking and defining the proper relations of the sacred records. Do we inquire as to the essential qualities of moral conduct, as presented in the sacred pages, in History, or in life? we have only to revert, as did our Saviour, to "the Beginning," our "Conscience"—"God within"—"the spirit in man"—"Inspiration of the Almighty" concurring in the *complete* and *unerring* solution.—All possible relations and conditions are easily referable to this epitome of natural rights and duties, in the order of the Creator's own establishment, wherein himself pronounced upon every department the clear, unequivocal character—"*very good.*"

Will it yet be claimed, a plenary dispensation in favor of Slavery is found in patriarchal example, and in the mere police regulations of the Mosaic economy? Why then condemn the "*Saints of the latter day,*" nestling and brooding in the mountain fastnesses and sinuous vales of Utah; there reviving the corruptions of the Israelitish saints of the *former day?* Why reject *any* custom or usage—some not here to be named—

which may have obtained by permission—not in the sense of indulgence, but "long-suffering"—"through the hardness of their hearts." A precedent has been established by our Saviour in the case of divorce; also in the law of retaliation. "But in the beginning it was not so." No precedent of higher authority can be found on Earth, or in Heaven; and it is, we believe, a well defined rule of law, that a precedent indubitably established, applies to all similar or analagous cases.

Ye Reverend Christian Doctors;—Jewish Rabbi too; behold the labored, tumulated chaff of your polemics, in apology or justification of American Slavery, scattered to the winds. "Not handling the word of God deceitfully, but by manifestation [declaration] of the truth, commending ourselves to *every man's conscience*, in the sight of God." As on Oath declaring, "*the truth, the whole truth, and nothing but the truth, so help me God*"—"*in the sight of God.*"

How cutting is the apt irony! "*Not handling the word of God deceitfully*"! Why omit the fact that servitude among the Jews under the Mosaic dispensation (for on some points not for ears polite it was indeed a *dispensation*;—not as "in the beginning"—) was generally voluntary;—a custom of stipulating service for an equivalent;—a system of hired service terminating with the sixth year, or at the year of Jubilee, with certain exceptions; but in no case as chattels common; a service to which the prodigal son aspired, "with bread and enough to spare"—"make me as one of thy hired servants;" (why not *slaves?*) Also its ameliorations, and personal rights, recognized and enjoined by positive law; "for thou too wast a stranger in the land of Egypt." And forsooth this is *Slavery!*

Surely ye will give us the *fugitive slave law;* ye will not "deceitfully" hide it. "O no, by no means," say these Doctors; "we have already given a *commentary* on this *fugitive slave law* in the matter of *Onesimus*," (a matter for our attention by and by) "but which for the present, *quantum sufficit.*" But as we have met many persons of average general intelligence, utterly ignorant of this *law*, we here give it; not requiring any, although we follow with a brief commentary :

"Thou shalt not deliver unto his master the servant who is escaped from his master unto thee. He shall dwell with thee, even among you in that place which he shall choose, in one of thy gates where it liketh him best, thou shalt not oppress him." DEUT. XXIII: 15, 16.

It cannot be maintained that this *"fugitive slave law"* was in favor of a *particular class* of *"slaves,"* for it is equally unjust, if unjust it be, to the masters of any and all classes. It is positive, and unqualified; while it is the only law for the *recovery!* of a fugitive. It is full proof of the benign and equitable policy, as to the relation of master and servant, and evidently intended to secure to the latter, complete immunity from cruelty and oppression. If it be alleged that it might injuriously affect the equitable rights of the master, in a given case; we answer: the master is fully aware of the custom and the *law ;* and the *probable wrongs without it,* very far exceed the *possible wrongs with it ;* a degree of perfection not always attained in legislation, and is therefore eminently humane, conservative, and just. A policy, this, widely different from that of American Slavery, in State legislation, and Supreme Court decisions; divesting the slave of all rights; and it is good logic—where are no *rights,* can be no *wrongs.* The Jewish code protects the weaker; the American, contrarywise to the utmost.

Will the Apologists and Advocates! of Slavery consent to the Patriarchal, the Jewish system, since on this they greatly rely to fortify themselves? Let them adopt the entire code, and since the customs of modern warfare do not enslave captives, it would be a glorious era of emancipation, neither immediate, nor very remote, but *sure.* An *Advocate of Slavery!* a moral *lusus naturæ* on *free soil,* until its recent *revival,* or *propogandism,* as by the sword of Mahomet, has multiplied its converts!

OF THE EGYPTIAN BONDAGE. The condition of the Hebrews in the "Land of bondage," Egypt, was that of a distinct community originally free, nourished and fostered, but by degrees reduced to vassalage by the oppressive exactions of the Monarch. In no manner did it correspond to the system of American Slavery. They were not the chattels of Egyptian masters—bought and sold; they had flocks and herds, and *dwellings too*, into which the destroying Angel failed to enter; and lived a distinct community in the land of Goshen more than four hundred years. (It was the boast of the Jew, "We were never in *bondage to any man*," of course *Slavery*, for the *nation* had been repeatedly in captivity.) With the exception of these Government exactions, operating most probably on a designated proportion or number of able bodied laborers, their condition would seem little changed, abating only from political favor.

The Romans, and other nations of Ancient times, enslaved at will their captives in war. This consequence of wars in those barbarous ages, was irrespective of race; and however absolute the subjection, it entailed no disqualification for freedom on generations unborn, nor indeed for elevated positions for the slaves themselves. It corresponded in absoluteness with the American, or even exceeded in the matter of life and death, (not practically we believe) while in many respects it was less intolerable and degrading.

It is, we believe, a comparatively modern doctrine of Religion, or Ethics, deducing the right of enslaving a *race*, of certain different complexion, if weaker or defenceless. Have we, by a strange inadvertence, overlooked any warrant for this in the original charter, "in the beginning"? Ah how blind and careless! how misled! self-satisfied by the fancied lessons of good will to man! through the Spirit within—"Inspiration of the Almighty!!" Well, the noblest reparation for *error*, is always a ready, full, frank concession to the *truth*. As we have already given a *part* (although we hastily supposed it the whole, and so made our deductions) of the original charter, we will now cheerfully complete the same; observing also by the way, that it must needs imply an exemption to the operation of the *fugitive slave law*, also already given.

'Eureka, GEN. I. 29. "And have thou dominion also over the weak and defenceless race whom thou mayst find in future ages (for with God thy Creator, the "Lofty One that inhabiteth Eternity," is no future) when thou art greatly multiplied, bearing thine image in outward form; of complexion neither white, fair, nor ruddy; nor of a red, brown, or yellow hue; but black as the blackness of darkness.

30. By this sign ye shall know, I have cursed that race by the mouth of my servant Noah, for the undutiful and irreverent behavior of him long aforetime their head and progenitor, which was Canaan, which was the son of Ham, which was one of the three sons of my servant Noah.*

31. Of this race thou mayest freely take unto thyself and to thy children, forever,—bond-men and bond-women, which with their seed, and their seed's seed, through all generations, shall be servants unto thee and thy seed forever.

32. And they shall serve thee; and thou, and thy seed, shalt rule over them.

33. And they shall be unto thee a possession; as thine ox, or thine ass, shall they be unto thee; even so also the fruits of all their labor shall be thine.

34. Thou mayest freely traffic with them, as with

---

* A convenient, but specious, unwarrantable, assumption of the apologists for Slavery; in self exculpation for the crime of creating the circumstances —not within "the third or fourth generation" but thousands of years after the original transgression, and within a comparatively brief period until the present time—yea, for the crime of wilfully creating the circumstances in fancied accordance with the supposed far-reaching curse upon Canaan, falling upon a remote (if the fact be so) posterity. Now it is historically true, that the descendants of Canaan were for ages distinguished among nations as the founders of Tyre and Sidon, principal cities—centres of civilization and commerce, of the then known world. Nor is there the shadow of plausibility, in the assumption of their descent—and still less, of verifying the prophetic curse, in the condition of slaves, made such by a nation calling itself Christian!

It is also historically true, that other nations—presumed descendants of Shem and of Japhet—grand nephews of their Uncle Ham, have in somewhat similar condition with their African cousins, been "held to service."

It has been reserved for the keen perspicacity of modern Doctors to discover the fulfilment of this prophetic curse, nearly four thousand years subsequently.

"For optics sharp it needs I ween
To see what is not to be seen."

merchandise, in exchange for silver and for gold, or for whatsoever else pleaseth thee.

35. If at any time they be refractory and disobedient to thy commands, and shall say "hath not one God created us ?" thou mayest *coerce* him or them by any means in thy power—by stripes, by scourging, or other painful inflictions, to duty and to entire submission.

36. And if he do not meekly receive thy reproof and correction, but becometh enraged so that he smiteth thee, or abscondeth ; his life shall be at thy disposal ; and none shall witness against thee ; thou hast not sinned.

37. And, as concerneth that race, I will annul my solemn ordinance of marriage, whereby a man and a woman, as it liketh them, are joined together in holy wedlock, that "they twain shall be one flesh" "until death us do part"—as is the authorized form and manner, concluding thus—"what God hath joined, let not man put asunder."

38. And thou mayest, instead thereof, use thy discretion, in order to increase thy possessions of bondservants, for labor, or for merchandise and traffic, nor shall the natural affection, by which the man and the woman careth for each other, or for their offspring, be made a hindrance to their separation by gift or traffic, as thy pleasure or need may require.

39. They belong not to each other, as thou and thy wife and thy children, joined, and begotten, in lawful wedlock, belong to each other ; but as thine ox, or thine ass, they are thy possession.

So readeth the missing portion, ten verses, following the 28th of the first Chapter of Genesis. This portion has been hitherto deemed Apocryphal, and ruled out as an uncanonical and incongruous interpolation ; but having been recently exhumed, in the exploration of the *latter day saints* (not alone of Utah) among the relics of the lost tribes of Israel, its genuineness can scarcely be doubted hereafter, and it has accordingly been restored in many churches of late, with approbation of Bishops and Pastors, that the evident deficiency of the canon may be supplied; thus relieving the pulpit from doubtful or questionable expositions. Its genuineness is strongly corroborated, if not established, in this, that the number of verses is same as of the lost tribes—*ten!!*

"A wicked, heretical interpolation," says the Orthodox divine.

"Evidently spurious," says the Biblical critic.

"Bogus!" says the frank, ingenuous, not over reverent, Ethical amateur Student, "with the preaching of Doctors P., Van D., *et id omne genus,*—all Bogus!"

If, indeed, it were an interpolation, it was certainly but a pious fraud, since it so perfectly harmonizes with the deductions of eminent Doctors of Divinity, whose expositions, *if true*, might well rest on so "firm a foundation" as is here in form presented, which we believe to be a faithful outline type of the *System* of American Slavery.

Ye Reverend Doctors, if ye judge this a wicked interpolation, suppress your indignation. Will ye *engraft* on the "Law and the Prophets" the abominations of Slavery, instead of the "Golden Rule" of Equity, emphatically predicated thereon by our Blessed Saviour himself: "Whatsoever ye would that men should do unto you, do ye even so unto them; *for this is the Law and the Prophets*"? The exact implied converse of this precept, equally binding, is clear: "Whatsoever ye would *not* that men should do unto you, do ye even *not* so unto them, for this is the law and the prophets." The great moral law of God is here meant, with the teachings of the prophets, of God's "*equal ways,*" versus man's "*unequal ways,*" and again summarily expressed by our Saviour: "Thou shalt love the Lord thy God with all thy heart, and with all thy soul, and with all thy mind. Thou shalt love thy neighbor as thyself. *On these two commandments hang all the Law and the Prophets.*" And who is thy neighbor? Every man in contact requiring aid, whether "*fallen among thieves;*" "*or in any trouble.*"

And yet will ye plead the Scriptures in justification of American Slavery? We can imagine but one mode of evading the common sense application of the "Golden Rule." It is substantially this: "With my present experience and knowledge," says the apologist, "of the conditions of mankind, were I a *black man*, I would prefer for myself and posterity forever the condition of Slavery to that of Freedom. So do I unto others as I would they should do unto me." Dare ye answer thus at the bar of God in the day of final account! at His bar who commands: "Break every yoke and let the oppressed go free"! Or will ye still plead the precedents of the *Jewish* statutes adapted to the exigencies arising from "the hardness of their hearts," "but not so in the beginning." Satan was a most adroit, *persevering*, scriptural casuist.

There yet remains one other plea, that of *necessity*, which we are quite willing to admit in its due force, and by which the *application* of general principles may rightfully be determined. It is said, "Necessity has no law;" and yet itself is a law; but not of immunity to those who *create* it, or *voluntarily strengthen* it, adversely to the great law of love and good will to man. While we discuss the *System* of Slavery, we pass no individual sentence upon the *slave-holder*. We charitably believe a very large proportion of such, from education, and life-long habit, unconscious participants in the wrong. While we do not hesitate to say of the *System*, with Wesley, "it is the sum of all human villanies," we do not thence assert the *slave-holder*, under any and all circumstances, a sinner *per se*, "above all others." It is the *animus* which imparts moral character to human actions; albeit in *human* law, the *animus* is inferred from the *act*. But God looketh upon the heart. A kiss may be "holy," innocent, affectionate, seductive, traitorous. So too the natural mutual complacency of the sexes, is the source of very innocent, refined, and elevating pleasure, (for we are no cynic) but of the seventh precept of the decalogue,

By a LOOK it is broken, if of impure desire—
When yet Purity's self, e'en to LOOK must admire.

But of *slave-holding*, whatever of *individual* sin it may be, is doubtless in the *intelligent consent* and *adoption*;

the *intelligent purpose* of *perpetuation* and *extension*. Perhaps few would plead for themselves the lack of intelligence, especially in this matter; and yet to many we accord it in charitable extenuation.

Nor are we ready to declare it—Slavery—but with qualification, *the national sin* of our common country; although in the organic law of our Government,—the Constitution; not from any purpose' of special favor, our nation became, very slightly indeed, committed to its protection in a special case; and that not materially affecting the stability of the institution; and only in compliance with a seeming temporary necessity. The continued existence, and the perpetuation, of the institution (for its *extension* was surely never originally contemplated by the Fathers of the Republic, but rather its *prohibition*) depended upon the policy and laws of the several States. Slavery, in its relation to our Constitution and Government, might seem to present a double aspect, first as accounted a national evil, for we know such has been the national tradition; and again with the semblance of guaranty for its protection; but this by no purpose of favor; hence so far, not chargeable as a *national* sin.

We verily believe, however, the Government of the nation, in all it higher departments, has been gradually seduced to a departure from its original proper character, that of conserving the interests of Freedom, until latterly, completely demoralized and prostituted, to answer the behests of Slavery. Thus, as of old, has Buchanan caused the American Israel to sin. Yet Christian Doctors—altogether ignoring this, dextrously showing *"how not to do it,"* deploringly present as on occasion of the late National Fast Jan. 4th, a vast aggregation of *individual* sins, as *national;* all which the laws discourage, condemn, and punish. These then, unless justified by public sentiment, are not *national* sins (See Isa. LVIII. ch. entire.)

Yea Verily, beyond peradventure, God hath a "controversy" with our nation. We have not taken away from the midst of us the *"yoke."* Greedy of national greatness, and jealous of foreign influence, we have claimed the lion's share, as pertaining to the American continent, under the guise of extending *Freedom* and civilization! but chiefly in latitudes for imposing the "*yoke.*" We have put forth the "*finger,*" yea, we have clutched with an *iron grasp,* ostensibly for just indemnity, but withal to strengthen and perpetuate the "*yoke.*" We have spoken "*Vanity.*" We have claimed and vaunted a van position in civilizing and evangelizing the world. We have said to the nations of the world, with reference to political, civil, social, and religious, institutions, as did Peter to the lame man at the Beautiful gate, "*Look on us.*" More than this—we have sent abroad navies for display of prowess. With lavish expenditure, we have *imported* from oriental climes, imperial delegations, chiefly to behold our *State ;* but who, when arrived, scarcely deigned, but with much appliance of tact at exhibition, to "look on us." We were *forcibly* reminded by the quiet self-satisfaction of these Japanese Heathen, how "easy it may be to lead a horse to water, but how hard to make him drink."

Yes, beyond a doubt, "God hath a 'controversy' with this people." The "groanings which cannot be uttered," of four millions of his children "*held to service,*"—*in perpetual slavery ;* with the *blood of martyrs* in vindication of the cause of oppressed Humanity ; of Lovejoy, and other like fearless asserters and defenders of Human rights—not including John Brown, of whom we only say, and this in no covert apology, "Judge nothing before the time." Yes—we do not hesitate to say further, if compelled to choose, as an only alternative—(and we bless God it is not so)—we would prefer the award of Heaven's Court, in that particular case, most decidedly would we prefer it, to that of the Leaders in rebellion and treason—the entire banditti—not excepting Bishop Polk.

Shall Bishops! *Priests!* and *Deacons!* *
Commissioned from above,

---

* Is it a fact—the characteristic CONSERVATISM (in its best sense) of the "Church" is sadly prostituted in sympathy with SLAVERY—REBELLION—TREASON ?!!! God forbid ! "From all sedition, privy conspiracy, and rebellion ;"—"GOOD LORD, DELIVER US!"

To light the way,—as beacons!
to *Realms* of Light and Love!
Shall such,—of holy calling ;
In van of *Treason* dare !
Nor give,—nor heed,—the warning,
Of Satan, to beware !
(From "The Old Flag"—better "*said*," than "*sung*.")

Leaving then John Brown with a just, yet merciful, God, and by no means impliedly justifying an open defiance and breach of *constitutional law, in any case ;* yet it is undeniably true, that devotion to a "higher law" than of human enactment, has vastly swelled the list of Holy Martyrs. The lion's den, the fiery furnace, the cross, the gibbet, and the stake, have been alike abundantly honored !!! We repeat,—the groans of Slavery, and the blood of Martyrs, by the score, or hundreds, perhaps thousands,—(and are there no blood stains yet visible on the floor of Congress—of the *Senate Chamber?*)—are witnesses at God's bar of unerring justice. Of the slave-trade and slavery, is it not pertinent to say—"the *times* of this ignorance God winked at ;" but after so long time of *exhortation* to "repentance," may we not fear—aye see—"*all is to be required of this generation*"!

(The further consideration of the New Testament, is reserved for second lecture.)

In this connexion we will venture, with little risk of judgment, to remark on the practicability of *ultimate* Emancipation, (not being of the *radical* abolition school, and these so few and widely scattered, as only to smoulder and smoke, whereas they must needs congregate to emit flame) based upon a policy of subordination. This question is indeed beset with *apparently* very formidable difficulties, augmenting with time. Why then delay the proper remedy ? No real evil is insuperable. "Where there is a will, there is a way." This rule is practical and sure. The first impediment, and often the most nearly insurmountable, is the lack of "a good will." We will not attempt to prescribe the particular measures to be adopted, but are confident we shall find God, in his wise Providence, guiding and "working with us when we have that good will." Phantom obstacles will have vanished; seeming mountains, become mole-hills.

"Like a wounded snake, it may drag its slow length along," but we feel it a moral certainty, that the first step in the right direction, will reach its glorious consummation—its goal—a United people, powerful, happy, and FREE. That *first step* is a change, or rather restoration, of National policy to its original programme (a step just taken, all *but* too late) followed by a *radical* change of State policy;—making Slavery the *subordinate*, instead of the *paramount*, interest of the people. Were this step taken by the *Slave States*, perhaps not simultaneously by all, but severally in succession, instead of their present disastrous and suicidal course of rebellion and treason; it would be the signal for a national feu-de-joy, from the Northern Lakes to the Gulf Coast; from the broad Atlantic to the broader Pacific; threading the rivers, and "raging canawls;" startling the hills, and waking the valleys; mountain to mountain echoing joy! O glorious vision! If aught could reanimate the sleeping dust, "or charm the dull, cold ear of Death," ere the final trumpet blast of the great Archangel; the mighty, honored dead, leaping from their quiet bed, of rolling years; revisiting the scenes of two centuries and more, from Plymouth Rock, to the far Georgian Shore; would swell the deafening, thrilling, cheers, of Freedom's Jubilee! But—"A change comes o'er the spirit of our dream." "Here endeth" our first Lecture.

List ye (in *parody*) to the "Spirit of '76":—

"Sons, for whom we fought and bled!
(We whom *Washington* oft led;)
Haste to arms, nor *traitor* dread!
Strike for Liberty!
Who for Government and Law,
Freedom's sword would strongly draw,
Freemen stand, or Freemen fa',
On to victory!

Now 's the day, and now 's the hour,
See the front of battle lower;
See array'd the *tyrant* power;
    Chains! and *Slavery!*
Lay the haughty *rebels* low!
Traitors fall in every foe;
Liberty's in every blow;
    Raise her banner high!''

'*Or this;*'' (Original.) Popular Music; by MASON.*
THE OLD FLAG. "*In hoc signo vincit.*"

  1. HUZZA!—for Freedom's banner!
    Let 's *cheer* th' red, white, and blue!
    "Star spangled" sign of valor!
    The Old Flag! Ever new!
    Our *Mothers* nimbly wrought it!
    Our *Fathers*, on the field,
    In Freedom's cause unfurl'd it!
    To win; but ne'er to yield.

  2. O'er hill top, plain, and valley,
    Its wavings greet the day;
    From shop, and field, they rally,
    Brave Freemen, for the fray;
    From city, town, and hamlet,
    On Freedom to attend;
    With rifle,—sword,—or musket,
    Her banner to defend.

(This third stanza "may be *said*, or *sung;*"—better
"*said.*"—Rubrical.)

  3. No Foreign foe confronts her;
    ("In Gath, ah! tell it not,")
    Fell Slavery defies her;
    Of record, *foulest* blot!
    Her own maternal bosom,
    The vip'rous foe, caress'd;

* We judge this familiar, popular, soul-stirring music, by MASON—AMER-ICAN in CHARACTER, as in origin, known as "The Missionary Hymn"—hap-PY POPULAR adaptation—even BETTER adapted to NATIONAL and PATRIOTIC use.

Till *bursting* with its venom,
The *Monster* stands confess'd !

4. Speed ! wind, and steam, our navies ;
Ye waves ! lend fav'ring tide ;
Ye Cars ! roll on our Armies ;
Ye Powers ! propitious guide :
On every sea-ward river ;
On soil,—on Ocean strand ;
Of victory,—THOU GIVER !
Extend thy Mighty Hand !

5. Who prays not—speed the battle !
'Gainst Treason's mad'ning rage ;
Pledging, 'mid cannon's rattle,
Unsparing war to wage !
No "*Compromise*"—with *Satan !*—
His most successful lure ;
But *crush* the rebel Ruffian,
And make the Conquest *sure !*

6. Then shouting "Hail Columbia !"
"Columbia ! Happy Land !"
"All clothed" in meet Regalia ;
Victorious !—Comrade Band !
'Tis yours, th' *acacia* bearing,
To chant—"*How sleep the brave !*"
In Freedom's rescue, daring
To win a PLUME !—or *Grave !*

LECTURE II.

NEW TESTAMENT TEACHINGS. NATIONAL AND SOCIAL INFLUENCE OF SLAVERY. ABOLITIONISM. "NEGRO EQUALITY." POPULAR ERRORS ON GOVERNMENT, &C., &C.

AFTER deciding, in our introductory Lecture, as we feel sure, the true bearing of the Old Scriptures,—of "the Law and the Prophets"—on the question of Slavery, with the KEY of our Blessed Saviour in hand —"*In the beginning it was not so ;*" and with the aid of His own "plain commentary"—"*Whatsoever ye would that men should do unto you, do ye even so to them ; for this is the Law and the Prophets ;*" we slightly digressed, to remark incidentally upon the general subject, from the direct line of the argument from scripture, to which we now return, more particularly to the New Testament.

We might trace a continuous chain of deductions abundantly warranted through the Gospels, in support of our position as to the *System* of *Slavery,* and wherein "nothing runneth to the contrary." We barely refer to the Sermon on the Mount ; to the Good Samaritan ; and briefly note "the Lord's Prayer."

"Our Father who art in Heaven." Then all we are brethren ;—heirs of a common inheritance. Cain, the first murderer, scorned the idea of *owning* the brother he slew. "Am I my brother's keeper ?" The brethren of Joseph debated sharply whether to *butcher,* or *sell* him ; and only adopted the latter, as an equivalent. Not being cannibals, they preferred the flesh of a kid for a repast. Later in the world's history an "elder Brother" was *sold !*—for thirty pieces of silver !

Every clause, of this divinely prescribed prayer, is equally suggestive of the same mutual, fraternal relations. Itself is ample theme for a *course* of Lectures, illustrative of these relations. Suppose we substitute the *singular*, first person, for the *plural*—*My* Father, &c. The wicked perversion would barely be equalled by its ridiculous absurdity. This doctrine of a common brotherhood is well exemplified in the Good Samaritan.

We scarcely need insist further on the general tenor and spirit of our Saviour's teachings, which altogether, as we have shown, utterly refute the baseless assumption of His *implied assent*, in not having specially reprobated the System; and this is the utmost gained by the most artful perversions, by the Advocates and Apologists of Slavery. But we deny to them even *this shadow* of argument. Our Saviour, as we have before intimated, on no occasion ostensibly set forth a complete *catalogue* of sins, for their formal name is Legion; yet all may be grouped under certain nomenclatures. Certainly he has not reprobated Polygamy, nor Concubinage, unless under the head of Adultery; or "in the beginning it was not so." But with Adultery, Murder, &c., He has classified *Theft*. Now we need not waste words to prove Slavery is the *most aggravated Theft*. We have shown clearly by God's own charter "in the beginning"—No man can of *right* hold property in man. No human law is valid which 'nullifies" God's law—original *Constitution—Supreme Law*. Again: he that stealeth a man, and selleth him, or if he be found in his hand, shall suffer death." Ex. XXI: 16. *Piracy is Theft, Murder*. The Laws of the United States, and of Christendom, have pronounced the Slave-trade equivalent to Piracy; its penalty, death. The *receiver* or 'purchaser* of a *stolen* horse, *as such*, is *particpes criminis* with the *horse-thief*, and thence a *horse-thief*. Let the stolen horse be sold, and resold, a hundred times over, to *innocent, bona fide*, purchasers; he is still the rightful property of the *original* owner, and must be restored. Thus no successive transfers, though in good faith, can confer more than the *original* right. There was an *original owner* of the horse, but *never* of the man. The parallel fails, *ab in-*

itio. The issue of the horse might be adjudged the property of the last purchaser, according to circumstances. Not so of the man. *He* was never *originally* rightfully *owned* by any other man, and no right of ownership can be acquired by mere transfer. To *seize,* or *withhold,* the just rights of another by robbery, force, fraud, or cunning, is *Theft.* Such is Slavery.

There are those who make, or affect, a broad distinction between Slavery and its origin—the African Slave-trade. They are horrified at the horrors of the "Middle passage," after the previous plundering of the weak and defenceless Barbarians, or inciting hostile nations to war for the sake of captives for traffic. But we confess our obtuseness to the logic which finds a moral distinction between them. The trite maxim, "the receiver is bad as the thief," applies here with equal force, certainly as to the voluntary participants, advocates, and abettors of Slavery.

And yet again there are those more consistent on this point, who make no distinction : in their PIETY! commending Slavery, with the Slave-trade too, as a *Christianizing* Institution ! What is the *motive* for this piracy and robbery ? Is it not to "fare sumptuously" without labor ? to amass wealth from unpaid toil ? to evade the sentence, "In the sweat of thy brow shalt thou eat bread" ? And then to insult High Heaven in this self-appropriation of credit, for doling just that *quality,* and *quantum,* of *oral* religious instruction, as may render the subject more serviceable. A christianizing institution verily ! Paying to a stolen *chattel,* made such by the theft, simply by adding to it a quality to enhance its chattel value ! "Go ye into all the world," &c., was the Commission ; or was it, "Except Africa," "Make slaves of Africans, deny them the Bible"—for its *fugitive slave law* would liberate them ; —but "compel them to come in." What self-deception ! "Be not deceived, God is not mocked, whatsoever a man soweth, [or a nation or people] that shall he also reap."

And this same is evidently about being fulfilled and verified in the present Southern Rebellion. "*Digitus*

Dei hic." " Quem Deus perdidit, prius dementat." Our adoption, in part, of the inspired lyric, will be no desecration:

> " God moves in a mysterious way, His wonders to perform;
> He plants His footsteps in the sea, And rides upon the storm.
> Ye patriot bands, fresh courage take, The clouds of gloom that spread,
> Are big with mercies, and shall break, In blessings on your head."
> The flashing gleams that ills portend, With rumblings distant far,
> The clashing peals that close attend, The thunderbolts of war,
> Shall purge the miasmatic air: Fair Freedom's sun shall rise,
> Her own majestic Eagle soar, In purer, brighter skies.

Recalled from a pleasing flight of fancy, we proceed to note, as before promised, the matter of Onesimus, to which has been claimed, and yielded, undue importance. What were the particular circumstances of this case, we cannot know. The inference, from the text, is fair, there were *peculiar* obligations, aside from the condition of servitude, otherwise, in remanding Onesimus to Philemon, (not as a *slave*," but a brother beloved,") Paul would have broken the law, had it been in Judea, under the Mosaic Law. This solitary case is "deceitfully" wrested to serve a false purpose, not intended by Paul, (a false precedent,) in this prudential compliance with the Roman Law, which, to his gratification, circumstances fortunately favored. The two—Roman, and Jewish—laws, because mutually opposed, could not both be *morally right.* The Roman was acquiesced in, from a Providential fitness (in which view we enter no protest against the *American,* so far as *Constitutional* ?) the Jewish, was *morally right,* because *merciful.* Did Paul remand Onesimus simply as a slave ? would he thus to a cruel master ? Paul, himself a prisoner of State at Rome, but privileged, would not needlessly jeopardize his opportunities of spreading the Gospel, by offending the laws of the Empire. "Be ye wise as serpents, and harmless as doves."

As to the precepts of the Apostle, touching the several relations of social life; among which is that of master and servant; these, as intended, are wisely suited to existing conditions and relations, on a basis of *reciprocity* and *equity.* Servants were enjoined to fidelity ; and masters, to render in return a fair equivalent—*"that which is just and equal."* By this, no law of the Empire was impugned ; and, as the principles of Christianity should prevail, any unrighteousness of laws would be abolished.

Christianity, as exemplified by its Divine Author, is eminently law-abiding ; and yet eminently and perseveringly protestant, in the strictest and best sense. It protests earnestly, unsparingly, against ; while it does not resist, evil, in unholy warfare. It endures, if need be, even to the death. It tolerates not the spirit of revenge. " Avenge not yourselves, but rather give place unto wrath." " *Vengeance* is mine, I will repay, saith the Lord." These, and similar precepts, distinguishing the lessons of Christianity, do not, however, repeal Nature's first law, hence a law of God, self-preservation; but are to be interpreted in consonance therewith ; yet, not to repel aggression by vindictive aggression—retaliation. The Scriptures are to be interpreted in the light of *reason* and *conscience.* We are alike commanded to " resist not evil ;" and to " resist the Devil." Literal, partial, and arbitrary interpretations, have given rise to these and other like characteristic and mischievous dogmas, Non-Resistance, and Transubstantiation.

In conclusion, on the New Testament, we find the word *"slave,"* but once in the whole Scriptures. It occurs in the enumeration of merchandize of the mystic Babylon—the mother of abominations, concluding the list with *"slaves, and souls of men."* Rev. xviii : 13. However innocent and lawful in itself, is most of this trafic ; yet is it an aggregation,— a *mammon*—of idolatrous worship, adding, withal, by climax, "slaves and souls of men." The natural, and correct translation, we think, would be *"bodies,* and souls of men,' the word rendered "slaves," primarily signifying the organic vitalized *body,* and by itself, properly rendered *"slave,"* if the condition so require ; but as here, the rendering seems tautological, for we deem *slaves* have *souls,* and whoever deals in *slaves,* deals in *souls,* inasmuch as the *soul* gives chief value to the *slave.* An idiot, or demented slave, would be worthless, except among cannibals. Corollary—If *souls* be *lawful* merchandize, then, logically, is that of *slaves.*

We have now taken a comprehensive view of the *system* of Slavery—our *target* both of sight and shot—from the stand-point of the Scriptures; and yet we have given but an outline definition of our subject. That outline, we believe, is truthfully drawn in the ten verses recently restored to the first chapter of Genesis, whether or not genuine, as before recited; and that it embraces, in its operation, all the *particulars* naturally pertaining to such outline is easily proved. But we will now more definitely, yet briefly, answer the question, What is *American Slavery?*

But, first, what it is *not.* It is not that *apparent* condition of comfort, and pleasurable occupation, which it is both convenient and desirable to present to visiting strangers, temporary sojourners, enjoying the hospitalities of the wealthy : Doctors of Divinity, in Ecclesiastical council at Richmond (alluding to the late triennial General Convention of the Protestant Episcopal Church of the United States, held at Richmond,) or Doctors of Democracy, in Political Convention at Charleston. As Christianity, so also, Freedom exerts a genial influence, casting a refreshing shade, and leaves of healing, beyond its own immediate pale ; and as none of the blessings of the former, are to be appropriated by infidelity and heathenism ; so none of the latter, are to be appropriated by Slavery as its *own,* while all *human* conditions partake of the ameliorations of Heaven's *own* Providence, overshadowing a common Humanity.

And, now, secondly, what it is It is an unmitigated outrage upon human *rights ;* if, indeed, the poor African be a *human being—a man* ; for it robs him of every *conceivable right.* Merely to *breathe,* is no *right.* To *breathe,* is to *exist—to be. Rights,* are *appurtenances* of *being,* by God's own charter ; and of all, and singular, the slave is robbed. Observe, again, we speak of *Slavery,* as distinguished from *Freedom.* Whatever is common to all estates of life, is not to be appropriated by

Slavery; for it is no part of *its* peculiar *System*. It is another specious and bold theft, in the very eyes, from the wardrobe of Freedom, to hide its own atrocious deformity. We pardon this theft, as of one reduced to starvation for bread. Prate no more of the comforts of Slavery, essential to life, and meted by a master. The *peculiar liabilities* of any condition, whether of a slave, or an ass, necessarily define that condition. True, we are referred to laws prohibiting cruelty. These are *conventional* merely, and precisely so are *animals* protected. The *slave*, no more than the *beast*, is a recognized *party*, at the bar of justice, or as *witness*.

Especially is the system a life-long robbery of the Creator's noblest endowments; otherwise, it could not exist, for "knowledge is power." In all other species of property, of the *animal* or *vegetable* kingdom, is sought the highest attainable degree of perfection. But in *man*, as *property!* ownership is less absolute, except as more cruel. It *dares* not cultivate the superior faculties. It dwarfs and brutalizes, the intellectual, and moral powers, to the limit adjudged by the master to subserve his interest. All religious instruction is to this purpose. In short, this is the settled, well-defined policy of the *System*. These prohibitions to mental and moral improvement, and of the rights of the *heart's* affections, are its *prominent hateful features*. Much stress is laid upon provision for physical comfort,—without which, a slave, as a horse, would be worthless. And yet there is a *"lower deep."* In contemplation of law, the condition is *perpetual*. It terminates with no "third or fourth generation." Notwithstanding the instinctive love of life, it contemplates hopefully the only gateway of release from its prison of despair,—the grave; where the "wicked cease from troubling;"—"and the servant [slave?] is free from his master." In vain, is the cry, with hands uplifted heavenward, " O Lord, my God, is there no help for the poor slave!" Echo answers, "none! none! none!"

. We may, indeed, draw a brighter picture, but it is, at best, only *accidental* to the System,--an extending of the hand of Freedom. We cheerfully concede that a race, peculiarly disposed to seek and find the means and occasions of enjoyment; with a native aptitude to be content and happy; will extract all possible honey of delights which the thistle-flowering field of Slavery may yield; and under favoring circumstances, where a genial humanity presides, may, for the time, be half conscious of the yoke. The *system itself* embraces *none* of the kindly sympathies of our nature, beyond the interest of the Master; such food and clothing, shelter, rest, and recreation, being allowed, as may suffice for this purpose. We concede more : that the *average* condition of the slave is quite above the *System* itself. It is undoubtedly felt to be the best policy to practice upon the slave a cheat, a deception, as if he were a *man*, to which his consciousness quickly responds; but the trader, the auctioneer, or the lash of the brutal overseer, as quickly dispels the illusion. To illustrate further : *Cannibalism* is not the capturing, guarding, feeding, or *fattening*—but the *eating* of its *victim.* So Slavery may not, cannot, utterly *exclude* all good; yet *itself includes "no good thing."*

We must not, however, omit the "*argumentum ad hominem,*" in exposing the wickedness of the system, and the absurdity of its clerical apologists—not to say defenders and advocates. We have occasionally seen both the white and the black man, in the sacred desk—alike arrayed in sacredotal robes—and together interchangably conducting the public worship of Almighty God. If "Slavery be not *per se*—sin—no not even in sense of original evil," why not disrobe the black man and reduce him to slavery, since to him, freedom is but a fortuitous boon, not an inherent right. It is only a question of power, or expediency, with the accidental difference of local jurisdiction, that the black man, in surpleic, may not the next hour be the common chattel of his clerical brother—the white man. Nothing but the unseemliness (with like incongruity) might prevent an immediate sale to the highest bidder, as of the seats in God's own house yearly, (for "the hardness of our hearts" a permission) under the hammer of the Auctioneer, if such an official chance to be present. We can scarcely imagine a slave market to be a greater desecration of God's own house—converting it to "a den of thieves," than the advocating, defending, or by apology, justifying the SYSTEM of American Slavery.

Let us now glance at the effects of the System of Slavery upon the dominant race. We would be cautious on this head, having little knowledge from personal observation.

First of the *Christianity*, and we assume to *judge* no man. To his own Master shall each one stand or fall. But we feel the prayer is appropriate. From the mock Christianity, which affects to worship with a brother, and kneeling by his side, "presses with his teeth" the symbolic "body," and applies to his lips the symbolic "blood of our Lord Jesus Christ," and will straitway arise and buy or sell, *for slave purposes*, that brother or sister, "image of God"—"temple of the Holy Ghost," as merchandise,—as an ox, or an ass;—from such Christianity, " *Good Lord deliver us!* " Judas did just this; nothing more! *"Inasmuch as ye have done it unto the least of these my brethren, ye have done it unto me."*

Enough of this picture. Next, of the *Humanity.* We here use this term, not in the *popular*, but the strictly legitimate, *generic*, sense, as comprising the dearest, most cherished, affections of our *whole* nature, but is enthroned in the *Soul.* What is it, which *virtuous* Humanity enshrines in its heart of hearts, scarcely less holy than his most devout aspirations heavenward ! (*Its abuse so much the greater sin.*) The allusion is sufficient. We wait no answer. It is intuitively recognized as the spring and source of noblest action, of most heroic endurance, and of purest Earthly joys, allied with holiest hopes; nor diminished, but purified, with lapse of years. The flame, inextinguishable by death, but brighter glows; wafting the soul onward and upward, to meet the loved ones gone before ! How dimmed then must be the fine gold of the God-given, God-like, Humanity, which, responsive to the law of its perpetuation, and immortality, blushes not, yea with shame-and abhorrence, for the *extreme* degeneracy that degrades to chattel inventory, as if of mere *brutish instincts,* a FELLOW MAN!!!

Why blush ye not to own kind Nature's law!
Why not "secede;"—from thy own *race* withdraw!
Asham'd to be a *man,* but *monster* be!
Or *man of prey,* as beast of like degree!
Slave trapper, hunter, trader, auctioneer;
Rearer, for mart!—and lash of overseer!!

This picture has two sides. "Look first on that side, then on this" following;—but modifying the one line of quotation from a celebrated poet:—

"Self-love, the spring of action, moves the soul,"
Rather, 'tis *self,* dispers'd among the whole,
Where love requites its like, and mutual joy,
Effort, and aid, this same self-love, employ.

All which, the slave *System* absolutely destroys!

In the third place: The System of Slavery begets the spirit of intolerance. Not only as regards an officious intermeddling, and overt interference, with the institution under sanction of law; (for it has little of this to fear from its most zealous opponents, under constitutional guarantees;) but, notwithstanding the boasted courtesy and hospitality of the South, it is unsafe to entertain conscientious opinions, adverse to the slave system, on slave soil. It has even the audacity to demand, that Northern sentiment, on this point, be corrected;—in other words—an efficient *gag-law.* We know this is its spirit; and had it the power, would enslave the *consciences* of Freemen. Free thought, and free speech, are banished from the region of its sway. The mails are violated. Constitutional guaranty of equal protection to citizens of the several States, is subverted. In place of argument—(which of course fails, as it well knows)— it adopts threats, menace, the bludgeon, the dirk, the bowie-knife, or the halter of Lynch law; while its more genteel mode of settling controversy, is by the chances of a pistol shot. All these equipments of personal assult are, in most of the free States, (in *all* of them, but to repel the aggressions of *Slavery*) unthought of in general society, even to be *scorned* and *denounced;* while in slave States, they are the common appointments, even of *Gentlemen!* Nor judging from the *tone* of some D.D.'s entirely discountenanced by them! in short, the *worst* features of Slave Society, are the legitimate results of the *slave System.* The redeeming features, (for it—the *System*—has none) are attributable to distinct, nobler, and in numerous cases we hope, to holier influences. We would not detract an iota from all that is praiseworthy in Southern character. Indeed it has ever been our habit, without personal observation, to associate with it, in our ideas, very much of the ennobling qualities of a higher humanity. Nor is it necessary here to estimate the exact degree of abatement from our former exalted opinion; from the late "awful disclosures" of *tyranny, rebellion,* and *treason,* unparalleled in the world's history. Say not, it is uncharitable to charge upon a wicked System its abominations, because necessarily implicating personal character. It could not otherwise exist, but by its piracy upon character, making its inroads upon the heart and conscience,—the fountains of character. It *sears* the conscience, and obscures the moral perceptions. Of Slavery, as of "Vice," substantially convertible terms, it is no less true—

It "is a monster of so frightful mien,
As to be hated, needs but to be seen;
Yet seen too oft, familiar with her face,
We first endure, then pity, then embrace."

In this connexion we adduce this further consideration: The *System* is not only a breach of the entire Decalogue, since it is authoritatively declared, "Whoso offendeth in one point is guilty of all;" and that it is Theft, is quite apparent, as we have already shown; the seventh precept of the Decalogue *is* also a quiver of arrows, to pierce its vulnerable heart: a very bomb-shell in its camp. It is admitted a cardinal principle in law—*quod facit per aliam, facit per se;* i. e., closely rendered "*Whatever one does through another*" by control, power, or direct influence, "he does *by himself;*"—makes himself the responsible agent, either as *principal,* or *accessory.* Now the *System* of slavery vitiates the sacred, indissoluble ties of lawful marriage. It utterly precludes this, whatever sham formalities may be indulged. Parents are separated from each other, as well as from their children, at the will of masters; necessarily f rming, or rather, *introduced* to, other spurious conjugal relations. The poor slave is but the involuntary, and therefore innocent, instrument—the *"per aliam;"* and the slaveholder, the *principal*—the *adulterer! "per se !"* It is also notorious that the CHURCHES !!! accord to the *System* a *plenary indulgence* in this matter, from the necessity imposed by the factitious! atrocious! dilemma presented !

Are not *fundamental principles* of Christian Morals unchangeable and eternal?—or are they, indeed, but accidental conventionalities? Modes of application, may vary; those, NEVER.

We next proceed to speak of the National influence of the System, Historically and practically, yet very briefly. Its pages *complete,* would fill volumes : and its more important points occupy a considerable portion of public records. We note a few points only, of immediate application.

The great moral truth is undeniable, first exemplified by the Serpent, in the specious temptation of our first parents, that all evil and sin gains lodgment, consent, and acceptance, by a covert and insidious policy. As on a certain occasion of olden time, so later, when the Fathers of the Republic came together to found a State, "SATAN *came also among them."* This is the unfortunate liability, against which no human undertaking has adequate security; though Washington, Franklin, and other like Sages, Patriots and Statesmen, be chief counsellors. The *virus* of evil is almost sure to be innoculated, which it may be nearly impossible to eradicate, nor easy to suppress; but if *nurtured* in the body politic, ensures disastrous results.

Thus was the *virus* of Slavery innoculated by the constitutional recognition of the system, as already existing in the several States ; yet declared to be a national evil, entailed upon the Colonies by the mother country, and which, with other causes, was boldly set forth, challenging the assent of the civilized world, as ample justification for *"Secession,"*—by the Mother, styled *"Rebellion;"* and by Historians, *"Revolution."* It is a remarkable fact, that the infant of that day now lives, when this *same cause,* or one of the causes of the *original "secession"*—this self-same cause alone, but reversing the terms of the plea, is declared the ostensible and only cause of a new drama of *"Secession."* The former causes, or one of them, that Slavery had been *planted* on virgin soil ; the present cause, that Slavery shall be *excluded* from Virgin soil. The Constitutional recognition of Slavery, as of "persons held to service," provided simply for a basis of taxation and representation, also the delivery of fugitives, "held to service," (the word *slave* purposely omitted as incongruous therewith) to the lawful claimants. In this recognition, Satan proved wiser than the children of Light, who doubtless contemplated its relative diminution, or ultimate extinction—a national evil—only to be endured, from a seeming present necessity ; as we know expressly condemned as such, by the fathers of the Republic ; and hence become the national tradition. Thus deluded by the *patron* of oppression, into a recognition of Slavery, he has perseveringly fostered it, under the various guises of the merchandize of the Mystic Babylon—"Mother of harlots and abominations of the earth," with whom not only "Kings of the Earth," (see Rev. xviii, entire,) but Presidents, and Lawgivers, have committed fornication ; and the "people have been made drunk with her wine ; conquering and coveting for the extension of her dominion ; and upon whom may be "found the blood of prophets and of saints," most abundantly shed.

And here we remark, the advocates of the system, by a strange fatuity, and perversion of right reason ; admitting the atrocity of its origin, charging it upon the *mother* country, as a national sin,—an introduction of evil; apply to the *turpitude* of the System, a moral series inversely to its *magnitude,* until, by this process of elim-

ination, its last infintesimal fraction has quite disappear-
ed. Now, it has become the corner-stone [see Appendix
—rebel Vice President Stephens,] of the State, on which
it is the avowed purpose to found an empire of unparalleled Glory. Yea, it is begun. The plan is fully
drawn upon the trestle-board, as a necessary prelimina-
ry, involving the destruction of Constitutional freedom,
as established by our Fathers. The gradations of Traitors—Masters, of several degrees, Fellow-crafts, and Ap-
prentices, under the vigilant supervision of the Roy
al Arch Traitor—Davis Jeff—(an approximation to
"*Abiff*") are at their tasks.

Hence have arisen false prophets, "calling evil good,"
"handling the word of God deceitfully," prophesying
deceits." For notwithstanding man's natural proclivity
to evil, it could make but slow progress in its own na-
ked deformity, a most sorry figure, of cloven foot, tail,
and horns; and only by its magic power of transforma-
tion; as of "an Angel of Light." "Blind leaders of the
blind;" throwing down their *professed* standard of the
Prince of Peace, and unfurling that of the Serpent,—of
Lucifer, in the van of rebellion, unparalleled since that
"son of the morning" marshalled his rebel hosts: as-
suring of "*religion's selectest influences*" (from a sermon
full of treason and rebellion, of an Episcopalian clergy-
man, delivered in Charleston, and repeated at Columbia
before the Magnates of *Slavedom*) and for success, invo-
king the "*god of battles*,"—*Mars*, of course.

The proper existing legal *status* of Slavery in the
United States, is plainly stated, to wit.: It is the foster
child of *Slave-State* law, born of oppression. Since the
law of any State has no force beyond its limits; it follows the bantling will die, unless restored to its proper
nurse. This, the Constitution, in a *specified case*, under-
takes to do; (rather forbids obstructions to recovery;)
but it provides no pabulum for its sustenance and perpetuation, in *voluntary* Exodus. If Slavery be of Divine institution, a positive good, protected by the National Constitution as rightful property, on principles of
"*common law*," this being based upon God's original, im-
mutable, law of *right*, as before shown; then is *slave*

property, everywhere, *rightful* property ; by the "Su·
preme law of the nation, the constitution and laws of
any State to the contrary notwithstanding." This evident *corrollary*, was recently boldly and plainly announ-
ced, in the *"bogus" constitution* attempted to be foisted
upon Kansas ; its preamble running somewhat thus—
(we quote from recollection): "Whereas the rights of
property are anterior, and superior, to all constitutions
or laws," &c. ; and assuming that slaves are *rightful*
property at *common law*, the deduction is perfectly plain :
No *constitutional prohibition* even, can be valid.

Practically, (and we appeal to all close and candid observation) the System of Slavery is the *Giant Evil* from
that prolific "root of all—that Pandora box—*"the love—
of money."* What but *the love*—of money, incites to
every hellish, murderous, depredation upon *Divinely*
human rights. What but this, emboldens the highway-
man presenting the *pleasant !* alternative—"your life, or
your purse." So the Prince of Highwaymen, Slavery
—robber of Nations—is already vainly essaying to throt-
tle with iron grasp, the most beneficent National Government upon Earth ; threatening destruction, unless acceding to his behests of supremacy. We fervently pray—
and who will not—Almighty God, to inspire the Heart
and Arm of our Government—both are strong in the
hearts of the people—to thrust, in retribution just, the
rebel fell,—though nurtured in its bosom, down to the
lowest —! But all subservient to the paramount prayer : "Thy will be done." Was it indeed for the *reign* of
Slavery, bootless struggle, that our Fathers bled ? bootless? nay, *not bootless,* "the boot is shifted to the other
leg." (The Mother Land is already free from the curse
of Slavery.) Was it not that *Freedom* should have a
home of right, and not by *sufferance,*—which is no *home?*
And shall we retrogade ?

With filial gratitude and just pride, we have been
accustomed to contemplate the Temple of Freedom, erect-
ed, though not completed, by our Fathers, at great cost
of blood, toil, and treasure ; the last a noble investment:
the first, a freewill offering, sacred to Patriotism. In
careful accordance with the plans already laid down

upon the "trestle-board," or harmonizing in order; we have continued towards its completion; wondrous for beauty and symmetry; adding column by column, united by its glittering, starry entablature, upon its wide-spread foundation. We have thought to transmit this, when the last Column shall have been reared, to the admiration of future ages; and we felt already beginning to realize the glorious vision of our own Native Bard melodiously apostrophizing—

"Columbia! Columbia! to glory arise."

When lo! to our astonishment and dismay, we behold an entire colonnade partly in ruins, dragging downward its tottering complement not yet fallen :

All tumbling, and crashing, nor *can* be replaced
In *original* beauty; but *sadly* defaced!

The catastrophe might have been predicted. It was well known to the Builders who laid and cemented the foundation; that under it, at this part of the Temple, was a substratum of quicksands—the quicksands of Slavery, which they erringly judged would in due time be-assimilated, by a natural process of petrifaction, to the adjoining rock. The Architects are conferring as to the practicability of "reconstruction;" aye, it is *undertaken* with a will;—God help the effort. The people are not slack. The *powers* are adequate, provided there be found a *firm* support for the *fulcrum* of the Archimedian Lever. This support can only be found upon the Rock of Freedom, however its Lever may extend beyond. We had supposed, as the difficulty of the quicksands is yet more insuperable than originally appeared, that it might be judged the wiser policy to postpone this project, in which the wisdom of our Fathers had so signally failed, untill a firm substitution for the quicksands may be effected. In plain language and dropping the figure, that while it is surely incumbent for the dignity and safety of the Government—the *ægis* of safety to the people, that wicked rebellion and treason be held to *strict account*, yet if neither honor, power, nor prestige, be lost; no dignity is sacrificed; when, by a SEVERE "*letting alone,*" the treason is impelled, *a la Japanese*, to the ultimatum of *hari kari—self-executioner.* Do we not hear the awe-inspiring mandate :—*"Ephraim is joined to his idols, let him alone!"* so, (as yelled the possessed of devils, "what have we to do with thee") echoes Rebeldom—"LET US ALONE!!!"

But the present energetic policy, foreshadowed in the President's inaugural, as now being more fully developed, is unquestionably the true—the *nobler* policy. A policy and example, due to the memory of our Fathers; due to the lovers of Freedom in all the world; due to the stability of all good government; due to Law and Order; due to ourselves and our posterity; due to future generations in *all* the world; due (by climax) to our own, and "Father's God,—Author of Liberty." Also due to all "lookers on in Venice" abroad or at home, who jeeringly point, taunting and vomiting, "there, there, so would we have it;" due to conspirators and traitors against free and good government in all the world, for all time; due to rebels and traitors at home; due—doubly due—again by climax—to Slavery and the D—l; for it is part of our creed, *"give the —— his due."* Last of all—due to the memory of the Signers of the Declaration of Independence; to the memory of the Battle-fields of the Revolution, — Bunker Hill — Ticonderoga—Trenton, Yorktown;—and later—New Orleans, aye and the *Hero.* Hark ye!—there is a rattling of dry bones at the "HERMITAGE"! The old *Hero* has "turned in his coffin!" Rebellion is aghast! The oath—*extra-constitutional,* in its awful sanction, rings in their ears—*"By the Eternal; the Union, it must, and shall be preserved!"* Aye—due, indeed, to New Orleans, in just retribution —but to the *Hero,* in HONOR; in Gratitude;—*"whom being dead, yet speaketh."* And finally, (another *last* climax)—due to *Washington,* the *Constitution,* and the *"flag of this Union,"* our own *"Star-Spangled Banner."*

*　*　*　*　*　*　*　*　*

"The Star-Spangled Banner, O long may it wave,
O'er the land of the free, and the home of the brave."

And now the Argument finds its Conclusion, in the *Ending,* or the "Beginning of the end," "of which we all are witnesses." And is it not fully conclusive of the real nature and sure tendency of the abominable sin of Slavery? Can that be a good thing which causes the ruin of a prosperous nation? On no other purely Moral question could arise such persistent clashing of *opinion*, and of *arms*: and it is as a *moral* question, hence *vital*, that it is invested with so great *political* importance; although many weak eyes can only look at the fiery meteor, shot from Slavery, through the murky, smoked, political lens, adapted to their own particular horoscope.

We are now prepared to propound what need not be discussed as the *finale* of our Argument. This present contest between Slavery and Freedom, in its *political proportions;* may be commensurate, not less, but threatening more, with our own Nation only: but, in its *moral proportions*, it is commensurate with the *World;*—coeval with *Time;*—lost only in *Eternity!* In battling for *Union*, Government, and Law, and for Constitutional Freedom, in this present struggle; all are campaigners in the Mighty Conflict between the powers of Heaven, and Hell: its final result not doubtful. Disguise it as we may, "the *irrepressible conflict*" between *Good* and *Evil*, is at our doors, unmistakably and hugely developed, in *Freedom vs. Slavery.*

Still one other argument, pro-slavery, we will not omit; deducing the *right*, from the *power* to enslave— i. e, "*might makes right.*" And this truly, as all know, is the only actual foundation for Slavery. Thus the condition of the Human race is made analagous to that of the winged, finny, or brute tribes; certain species being carniverous, beasts of prey, duly equiped by Nature for this purpose. This analogy may be traced, as presumed, in the natural antipathy of color, wool, and other like accidental discrepancies; and again, in superior cunning in the application of physical agencies, instead of *ferocious claws.* So the inferior, or defenceless, condition of the African, clearly indicates him, as "lawful prey"! This is really the *best argument*—pro-slavery, that human ingenuity can devise. We will be fair; we will not be partial; but give both sides. Both arguments are equally comprehensive: the one, "*In the beginning it was not so;*" the other, "*Might makes right.*" "If the Lord be God, serve him; if Baal, serve him." "Rightousness exalteth a nation; but sin is a reproach to any people."

Having concluded our argument, we will yet add a few wards supplemental; lest the "hue and cry" of "mad dog" be raised, inviting a stone---hard name--- from every *pseudo* Unionist.---"Abolitionist"! "Black Republican"! "Negro Equality"! &c., &c., &c. We know also these terms mean the same, both North and South, though somewhat intensified at the South by a characteristic epithet, as "d---d Abolitionist," &c. For ourselves, we fear not; but our "*child*" we will guard and protect. We will not leave "Truth to be evil spoken of."

First then, we are an *Emancipationist*, precisely as was Washington; "*it being among my first wishes* (wrote he in 1796) *to see some plan adopted by which Slavery in this Country may be abolished by Law.*" Call ye Washington,—Abolitionist? We share the reproach joyfully. We stop not here to add from the same, and a score of other like names, concurring repeatedly and heartily, in the same noble sentiment.

"Negro Equality." On this point we shall be equally explicit, though necessarily more extended. This slanderous imputation has reference, of course, to social, and civil or political *status ;* (mere *natural, personal*, endowments have no relevancy; for *these* are unequal, in *either* race) and results from the radically false, popular theory, on Government; which, but for ignorance, or inconsideration, or erroneous education, would also be impious. We do not believe, without warrant, (and we have none) in "the Divine *right* of Kings, but we have, no, not the slightest, objection to "Victoria, *by the Grace of God*, Queen.

God, is the Supreme Ruler, as the Creator, of the Universe. *Governmental Power and Authority* are *inherent* only in Him. "By me Kings reign and Princes decree justice." We do believe in the *Divine Institution* of Civil Government; whether by Kings, Empe-

rors, or Presidents; or other Magistrates mediately
chosen by the people. We believe a *pure* Democracy
impracticable.

To make this quite clear, as of other truths before
treated, we again revert to the "Beginning." God
gave man no "*dominion*" over himself, or his fellow-
man; neither of rule, nor of proprietary right. He
did not say to man, "Thou art free and independent."
A conscious *freedom* was indeed imparted in "the
breath of life," by which man became a living soul;
and also a subject of Moral Government; but not *Independence*. Freedom, and Independence, are really
quite distinct, although germain, as concerning equals.
God Himself is King proper. All else are but *vice-
gerents*, by His Providence: "*Dei Gratia*"—"By the
Grace of God." As, "by the *Grace* of God, I am what
I am."

The *true* theory of Government, among men, is that
of *Divine Wisdom*, through human instrumentalities.
The *Theory* is the same, under whatever form. The
form, either submitted to, or chosen, by the people, is
by God's providential direction, or permission. The
problem for solution, so far as human agency is con-
cerned in the adoption, is by what form may the *Divine Wisdom* be most largely and practically secured;
practically, with reference to the varying conditions
of Nations, or Peoples.

We think it not necessarily true, if generally, that
"What'er is best administered, is best;" the *form*
being Providentially adapted to the habits or genius
of the people, and best, as best adapted. A heredit-
ary Monarch, specially educated for this end, may be
as *good*, and as *wise*, as any one of his subjects; and
therefore, as all of them together; or he will profit by
their counsels. The character of a *Popular* Government may be estimated *good*, as the people are *wise*
and *good*; and being a reflex of popular opinion and
sentiment, its best security is the collective *wisdom*
(not folly) of the people—the proper basis of the Elective Franchise; excluding, as far as possible, all un-
worthy elements. The prerogatives of human agency

in Government, should be accounted as only appropriate to intelligence, virtue, and patriotism. A *popular,* is not necessarily the *freest,* Government. The broadest latitude of franchise, may be but the worst tyranny of Ignorance, Prejudice, and Vice.

Kings, Emperors, Presidents, Parliaments, Congresses, Magistrates of every grade, Law-Makers, and Law-Executors; also *Electors;* all are but the *Machinery* of Government, chosen, or allowed of God in His Providence. It is a miserable self-deception—a mischievous cheat—the political cant—*"Sovereign people"*—a mere atheistical ideal abstraction. Look at it —Sovereign, without subject! or *idem*—Sovereign and subject! No place for allegiance, nor treason. Nor are the people exactly unconscious dupes of the cheat; they feel it so: Aye, self-judged, "but very clowns in regal purple dres'd." In difficulties, seeking *higher* wisdom; in perils, as of late, will they cry mightily unto God, "Save Lord, or we perish." Note how, as by an instinctive reverence, with uncovered head, and respectful tread, we all approach the seat—the repository—invisible Shekinah—of Judgment and of Power, though the *agent* be one of *ourselves.*

We have before said, and who will deny, that the Creator—God—is the only King proper, in Whom only the *right* of Government *inheres ;* hence all instrumentalities—the machinery of Government—are by His express, or Providential, delegation. No *right* of Government inheres by orig'nal investiture in Man. We here distinguish between *rights inherent,* as originally and equally devised; and *privileges delegated,* involving necessarily correlative duties. Instrumentality in Government, (an elevated position truly, of which, in the popular form, the *Elective Franchise* is the primary step,) is, under God, by *special delegation* and *qualification.* That certain qualifications are prescribed requisites for official honors, and duties, and for the privilege of the *Elective Franchise,* works no injustice to others, excluded for lack of such qualifications; for no *rights, inherent* and *personal,* are infringed ; and no privilege, or franchise, has been wrested, or withheld ; for none such had ever been delegated, or conferred.

The civil, or political franchise of Elector, is not identical with that of citizenship ; yet *both* are properly by *judicial* discrimination. So a foreigner, of any Nation, may be rightfully excluded forever ; or a discrimination among these may be rightfully made ; as between Europeans and Asiatics ; or Africans and their descendants. No one never *Enfranchised,* can be *Disfranchised.* Equal *subjection* to law, and equal *protection,* are equal *rights.*

At the risk of incurring the charge of repetitious, we will yet extend these remarks. Our object is to impress the subject on the mind. Even a *lie,* it is said, gains credence by repetition ; and *truth* is vastly more worthy the pains.

Very erroneous conclusions have resulted, sometimes with evil effect, in not properly discriminating between *inherent personal rights,*---the same essentially in all persons ; and *accidental privileges,* imposing corresponding *duties.* The *personal rights* of the humblest citizen, are precisely equal to the *personal rights* of the Chief Magistrate of the State, or Nation. To be an Elector, is not a *right,* but a *privilege.* This distinction seems accurate, though the two be generally confounded. Privileges are necessarily diverse and accidental ; not strictly personal, or only so, as the person answers to certain prescribed requirements, or qualifications. "There is one glory of the Sun, another of the Moon, another of the Stars ; and one star differeth from another star in glory." So is it in the *accidental,* or *Providential* (the same) conditions of mankind. Governments are special repositories of Power, (*"where the word of a King is, there is power,"*) of which God is the source. He delegates power, through his Providence, in such varieties of modes, and to such *classes of agents,* as He wills.

Qualifications, of Property ; of Education ; of Birth ; of Age ; of Residence ; of Character ; of Race ; of Color ; of Nationality, &c., are prescribed by the POWER. Government, and its machinery, are not for the purpose of *personal* honors and emoluments,---but for *general secunity, and welfare.* The Power which excludes from the Chair of State, may rightfully exclude from the Electoral Franchise. A *claim,* of *right,* to the *Franchise,* is equally strong, to the *Chair.*

Let no man then, of whatever *race,* or *color,* enjoying equal common protection, feel it a grievance that he is accidentally debarred the privileges, and relieved from the responsibilities and duties, of *Political* Citizenship, and of the Electoral Franchise. "But," says the ambitious aspirant, "am I not equally taxed?" "Very well, you are also equally protected." "But," it is rejoined, "was it not against taxation, because not coupled with representation, that the American Colonies protested?" "Admitted;---but the Colonies, not being integral portions of the Realm, at the same time renounced her *protection.* It would have been at best but a very *lame* plea or ground of complaint, if, with no *excessive* burden, they had continued to claim, and receive *protection.* They demonstrated the revolutionary right (by the power to enforce it) to *protect* themselves, and for this, to *tax* themselves; and you, too, my colored friend, my equal in *personal rights,* may renounce protection, and of course, avoid its consequent burdens: how?---by Expatriation." The body *politic,* by its peculiar functions of rule and direction ---affecting all the ramifications of Society, does not therefore necessarily *incorporate* in itself all these; but clearly illustrates the distinction it would maintain, in the great exponent of its Power---the Organization of the Military Arm. It subjects, and protects, indiscriminately; relying for defence solely upon itself.

The same general principles rightfully obtain in Social life. A family is a miniature body-politic, with its conditions of membership, and of intimate, or general, social intercourse.

Let it then be clearly understood, neither equality of civil, nor of social, *privileges,* are, necessarily, *inherent, personal rights.* A distinction of race, is a *natural barrier,* which it is no unjust prejudice to acknowledge and regard; yea, it is, we are sure, a *duty* to maintain;

and none the less duty because involving relative, *due* subordination, which after all is less real than apparent, each in its proper place. The *social* and *political* disadvantages of the African race, can only be remedied by *colonization*, i. e, gathered in distinct communities. "Negro Equality" is but the Quixotism of a spurious Philanthropy. Interspersed among the dominant race—by far the wiser course is to be content in "the cool sequestered vale of life."

> "Honor and shame from no condition rise;
> Act well your part, there all the honor lies."

This disposes of the slander—"*Negro Equality.*"

It follows clearly from this reasoning, to define the idea of *allegiance*, and the wickedness of *rebellion and treason.* Both these have like primary relation to the seat—the repository—of supreme national power. *Allegiance* can only be predicated, as *due* to *Nationality.* Its undeniable counter-claim is *universal protection.* The national flag is the symbol and seal of this mutual relation. A subordinate or divided allegiance! Allegiance to a mere *body politic* divested, or destitute, of all proper attributes of nationality, is a *ridiculous absurdity.* It is time this too prevalent, and *really mischievous*, fallacy were exposed. Born in Connecticut, our good old "land of steady habits"—"nutmeg State" —(for it is indeed among, if not chief of the spices which flavor our cup of "thanksgiving," of life and joy)—but for a time resident of other States; we would as soon make oath of *allegiance* to one, as to another *free* State—a sham in any such case, without distinct, *complete, nationality. Allegiance is due only to my country.* True loyalty is willing, prompt, decisive. It disdains an equivocal position. Treason only is equivocal. "I would thou wert either cold or hot, but as thou art neither cold nor hot, but luke-warm; I will spew thee out of my mouth."

It follows, too, (admitting, as correlative, that "*resistance to* TYRANTS *is obedience to God,*") that rebellion and treason against a *benign and paternal Government,* are crimes of the blackest dye,—rebellion and treason against GOD'S THRONE. "*For there is no* [rightful]

*power but of God : The powers that be are ordained of God.
Whoever therefore resisteth the power, resisteth the ordinance
of God : and they that resist shall receive to themselves
damnation.*" And how determine the validity of power ? Generally by another simple rule of our Saviour,
" *By their fruits ye shall know them.*" We *need* not err,
though unaided by the exact sciences. Let D. D's, Bishops and Pastors, who *dare*, pervert these Scriptures
to the support of THE GREAT REBELLION !

This closing remark seems also pertinent to our general position, on Civil Governments, to wit : the evident *fallacy* of the favorite political dogma, that of
"*Governments deriving their just powers from the consent
of the governed.*" This proposition befits no *Government*
at all. A political paradox,—illogical,—unphilosophi-
cal. It is most completely illustrated in the present
rebellion, of which it is a complete justification.
Nothing is more essentially *true*, than,—the duty of
obedience to Government and Law, is independent,
and irrespective, of *Consent.* The proper Exponent of
Eternal Justice, waits for no consent. It does not pre-
face its edicts—" by your leave." The only *consent* required of Adam was *obedience.* His dissent, or rather
disregard, cost him his earthly Paradise. *Consent* im-
plies the right of *dissent.* Although seemingly plausible, yet is it a political Heresy—another proof that
"*great men* are not always wise :" and *good* men are fal-
lible. " To err is human."

IN CONCLUSION :

We are constrain'd to admit, in humliation,
Ere twelve moons had passed, lo ! this is the nation,
In the pride of its strength, made itself an ovation,
High vaunting its power and its civilization,
Before the Almighty, in face of creation,
Making show to the Heathen, its vast exaltation ;
Repeating the like, though with less affectation,
In Royalty's presence, with renewed exultation ;
Nor "took God for its strength" but self-elevation ;
("Like people, like priest," an apt illustration,
At Slavery's *shrine* their only prostration,)
Now, brought to the verge of annihilation ;

Its grievous oppression, the true provocation
For Heaven's chastisement, in just dispensation.
Let us fervently pray, in deep supplication,
O Lord, turn away thy just indignation;
May repentance avert the sure publication,
On History's page, of the worst condemnation.
Now trifling no more in loose versification,
On a subject too grave for light alliteration,
With the bright star of hope, from deep obscuration,
Emerging in radiance, to cheer our probation,
Unite we our voices with rapt animation,
In *genuine* Lyric, of rare adaptation.

  " My Country, 'tis of thee,
  Blest Land of Liberty,
   Of thee I sing !
  Land where my fathers died ;
  Land of the pilgrim's pride ;
  From every Mountain's side,
   Let Freedom ring.

  " Our native Country, thee,
  Land of the noble, free,
   Thy name I love!
  I love thy rocks and rills ;
  Thy woods and templed hills ;
  My heart with *rapture* thrills,
   Like that above.

  " Our Father's God ! to Thee,
  Author of Liberty,
   To thee we sing !
  Long may our Land be bright,
  With Freedom's holy light ;
  Protect us by thy Might ;
   O God,—our King !"

Or this :—" *The Good Old* CONSTITUTION." [Orignal.]
Tune : Now rambling afield, here's a *gem* aptly fitting,
Just suiting our measure (*omitting first strain**)
Transferr'd to our vase, though less daintily sitting—
The *Air* of "Sweet Jessie, the flower of Dumblane."

---

*First strain may be played as an interlude.

Song: How cherished in mem'ry the way-marks of story
As struggled our fathers in unequal fight—
Now yielding, now gaining ; thro' suff'ring, to glory ;
Till our Old Constitution, mid cheers hail'd the light.
Chorus : The New Constitution, good Old Constitution;
Till our Old Constitution 'mid cheers, hail'd the light.

On the *kirk** glebe of Lexington, hallow'd by pilgrims;
On Bunker's proud height where a Warren first bled—
A martyr to Freedom ; of strife the beginnings,
To the New Constitution, through vict'ry, that led :
Chorus: The New Constitution; good Old Constitution;
To the New Constitution, through vict'ry, that led.

At Ticonderoga, at Monmouth, at Trenton,
Unwav'ring, unflinching, intent on the prize ;
At Yorktown, last winning; Independence full bent on,
And the New Constitution to gladden our eyes.
Chorus. The New Constitution, &c.

But first, a " *Confed'racy*"—ominous trial ;
For proving loose rein, in the National race ;
So they left to "*Secession*" the dregs of its vial ;
And the New Constitution, ordained in its place :
Chorus : The New Constitution, &c.

As mariner watching the sure-guiding pole-star ;
Or with quadrant right pois'd, after clouds, takes the
  Sun ;
Or as beacon-light gleaming, in night-darkness seen far,
So the New Constitution insures a safe run.
Chorus : The New Constitution, &c.

As bridge of hewn rock, on its key'd arches resting,
More firmly sustains, as more heavily press'd ;
So our Old Constitution we'll cheer with a blessing ;
Safe bridge of a Nation, by Nations confess'd :
Chorus : So our old Constitution, let's cheer with a
   blessing ;
Good Old CONSTITUTION, by Nations confess'd !

Riddle : Now ask ye the *rhymer?* this riddle may show it;
Who recklessly snatch'd up the mantle that fell
From his namesake, so gracing the *genuine* Poet
Of the " *Old Oaken Bucket, that hung in the well*"?

---

*The field showing the characteristic picture of the Puritan Church.

APPENDIX.

TESTIMONY.—We designed to give a *few samples* of the *many* protests against the System of Slavery,—of those best acquainted with its conditions;—of men whose sterling integrity and honor (and therefore "worthy of double honor") were proof against its debasing influence. Such may be numbered by dozens, scores, or hundreds, but not to exceed prescribed limit, we present one additional; — Washington, already "*first*"—as "in war"—"in peace"—"and in the hearts of his countrymen."

We here adduce Jefferson—honored name, inseparably identified with the Declaration of Independence, Apostle of Democracy—*as it was.*

From his " *Notes on Virginia:—*

" There *must be* an unhappy influence on the manners of our people, produced by the existence of slavery among us. The whole commerce between master, and slave, is a perpetual exercise of the most boisterous passions—the most unremitting despotism on the one part, and degrading submissions on the other. Our children see this, and learn to imitate it ; for man is an imitative animal. This quality is the germ of all education in him. From his cradle to his grave, he is learning to do what he sees others do. If a parent could find no motive, either in his philanthropy, or his self-love, for restraining the intemperance of passion towards his slave, it should always be a sufficient one, that his child is present. But generally it is not sufficient. The parent storms, the child looks on, catches the lineaments of wrath, puts on the same airs in the circle of smaller slaves, gives a loose rein to the worst of passions, and, thus nursed, educated, and daily exercised in tyranny, cannot but be stamped by it, with odious peculiarities. The man must be a prodigy who can retain his manners and morals, undepraved by such circumstances. And with what execration should the statesman be loaded, who, permitting one half the citizens thus to trample on the rights of the other, transforms those into despots, and these into enemies ; destroys the morals of the one part, and the *amor patria* of the other ; for if a slave can have a country in this world, it must be any other, in preference to that in which he is born to live and labor for another ; in which he must lock up the faculties of his nature ; contribute, as far as depends on his individual endeavors, to the evanishment of the human race ; or entail his own miserable condition on the endless generations proceeding from him. With the morals of the people, their industry is also destroyed ; for, in a warm climate, no man will labor for himself, who can make another labor for him. This is so true, that of the proprietors of slaves, a very small proportion, indeed, are ever seen to labor. And can the liberties of a nation be thought secure, when we have removed their only firm basis —a conviction in the minds of the people that these liberties are the gift of God ; that they are not to be violated, but by his wrath? Indeed, I tremble for my country, when I reflect that God is just ; that his justice cannot sleep forever ; that considering numbers, nature, and natural means only, a revolution of the wheel of fortune, an exchange of situations is among possible events ; that it may become probable by supernatural interference ! The Almighty has no attribute, which can take side with us in such a contest."

Again :

" We must wait with patience the workings of an over-ruling Providence, and hope that that is preparing the delverance of these our brethren. When the measure of their tears shall be full ; when their groans shall have involved Heaven itself i darkness, doubtless, a God of justice will awaken to their distress. Nothing is more certainly written in the Book of Fate, than that this people shall be free."

Is this prophecy now being fulfilled!

In a letter to James Heaton, on this same subject, dated May 20th, 1826, only six weeks before his death, he says :

" My sentiments have been forty years before the public. Had I repeated them forty times, they would have only become the more stale and threadbare. Although I shall not live to see them consummated, they will not die with me."

Much more might be quoted from the "sage of Monticello." Nor is the voice of Madison, of Monroe, of him of "Roanoke"—of his namesakes—four Randolphs of "Virginia's sacred (to slavery? or for Yorktown and Mount Vernon!) soil" Alas, how desecrated ; also of Clay, of Benton, of Mason, of McDowell, of Pinckney, and others too numerous to mention, by far to *quote ;*—wanting, in equal terms of condemnation. In exact correspondence with these, the common-sense argument presented in our Lectures, of the debasing influence of Slavery. And is not this *closing warning* awfully *prophetic* ? God's "Spirit in man"—Inspiration of the Almighty—often finds utterance, distinct and clear, however unconscious the medium. Nor are the *greater* and *minor, political* prophets few. Behold they are gathered—(not all)—in "The Impending Crisis." We name this for facility of reference merely. Nor are its unanswerable arguments to be refuted—its home thrusts, to be parried, by ungenerous criticism of style or manner, which, so far as obnoxious, is but itself an argument against the System, as both *meriting,* and *engendering, harsh* condemnation. It was not we presume designed as a model of etiquette, and punctilious regard to the nice distinctions and delicate manœuverings of the "*Code.*" It is not the *plaster ;* but the *probe.*

And are not these prophetic testimonies now being fulfilled? "Out of thine own mouth will I condemn thee." "Wicked Monster;"—"Sum of human villanies:" all detestable names in one :—Liar, Thief, Murderer, Adulterer, Pirate, Traitor, "Vile and impious Ruffian wretch"—Slavery! "Hold up your head and hear your sentence:" "As you have done unto others ;—so shall it be done unto you." "Ye ministers of wrath! see that these penalties are executed!" War! Pestilence! Famine! The *first,* may complete the work; may the *latter,* be stayed!

The Car of inexorable Justice is moving, which only the marauding *imps,* in guise of *Conservatism,* or of *Compromise,*—specious, *stolen,* names,—may temporarily jostle from the track; but will ultimately crush, and sweep away, "the great offence."

Conservatism!—Compromise!—*Umbrellas* for occasional showers: stolen from the outer porch of "Wisdom's *own* house;" (Prov. ix: 1.) Already in tatters from misuse. Miserable shelter!

Conservatism!—Compromise!—milk cataplasms. applied to gangrene and putrefaction: the *soft solder* of the wily trickster. Inefficient as ye are—mere time-servers —temporary expedients—we turn for a moment to the rescue, as we pass; snatching from the base *purloiner* his ill gotten appliance, and leaving to *himself* the *onus* of complaint at Court.

First ;—*Conservatism,*—is properly applicable, only to "whatsoever things are true ;"—"honest ;"—"just ;"— "pure ;"—"lovely ;"—"of good report ;"—to all of "virtue," "praise," and "godliness of living."

Second;—*Compromise*—can be properly presumed, only in relation to matters indifferent: i. e., involving no *moral* principle whatever. It is no balance in the scale of *Justice*. It is no element of *Truth*. Nor is it the handmaid of *Love*, or of *Mercy*. If by it any of these are affected, it is injuriously, as pure gold by alloy of baser metal. It is simply an unwilling yielding of what is not easy, or safe, to retain of contested proprietary right. But the proper individual *rights* of no man, conflict with those of another. "*Society*," then, with all deference, (meeting a plausible assumption) "is not a *compromise*, and rests upon no such system." Rather, is it not the tinkering of "*Compromise*," which is the sure, slow-match to the "magazine of explosive elements (?) composing society?" Nor yet is Society but a compact for mutual aid and protection, though admirably serving this purpose; but *God's own* Institution, conserving, (and this is His conservatism) its best, highest, interests; and hereby enhancing, not diminishing, each individual interest. Man is eminently a *social* being; and the fold —the shelter—of Society, demands no "*Compromise*," although it forbids *trespass*. The great end of society is, that we may be fellow-*Helpers* in all *good* works, upon Earth; introducing to the Society of the "just made perfect in Heaven;"—while mediately, it "serves to second to some other use" in conserving, and preserving, *entire*, all of *right*, and *equity*, among men. Where is the *Compromise?* Thus much for the talismanic virtues of these *panaceas* for social or private ills.

THE OTHER SIDE OF THE PICTURE.

" The foundations of our new government are laid. Its corner stone rests upon the great truth that *Slavery*—subordination of the inferior race, is the natural and normal condition, of the negro. This, our new government, is the first in the history of the world, based upon this great physical, philosophical, and moral truth."--*Rebel Vice President Stephens.*

A radical fallacy here. *Slavery*, and *subordination*, so far from being synonymous, and convertible terms; are by no means necessarily related, or cognate; but really distinct and opposite. The one—*subordination*—indicates a prominent truth in the Divine economy of the Universe;—and includes in every gradation, specific peculiar rights and immunities; the other—*Slavery*—completely subverts, and robs of all!

The latter clause also—"this, our new government," &c., repudiates, as illegitimate, the favorite pro-slavery argument, to wit: *Slavery, coeval with History;* propounding in terms,—"*the physical, philosophical, and* MORAL truth, that "Slavery" "is the natural and normal condition of the *Negro*," and yet a corner stone of Government never before laid in "the History of the World." The *ne plus ultra* of political wisdom!

We will now present the letter of Charles O'Conor, acceding to the request of his speech for publication, by distinguished merchants of New York :---the advocate of *Simon pure,* National Democracy, *par excellence :---*

GENTLEMEN :—The measure you propose meets my entire approval.

: I have long thought that our disputes concerning negro slavery would soon terminate, if the public mind could be drawn to the true issue and steadily fixed upon it. To effect this object was the sole aim of my address.

Though its ministers can never permit the law of the land to be questioned by private judgment, there is, nevertheless, such a thing as natural justice. Natural justice has a divine sanction; and it is impossible that any human law which conflicts with it should long endure.

Where mental enlightenment abounds, where morality is professed by all, where the mind is free, speech is free and the press is free, is it impossible, in the nature of things, that a law which is *admitted* to conflict with natural justice, and with God's own mandate, should long endure?

You will all admit, that within certain limits, at least, our Constitution does contain positive guaranties for the preservation of negro slavery in the old States, through all time, unless the local legislatures shall think fit to abolish it. And, consequently, if negro slavery, however humanely administered or judiciously regulated, be an institution which conflicts with natural justice and with God's law, surely the most vehement and extreme admirers of John Brown's sentiments are right; and their denunciations against the Constitution, and against the most hallowed names connected with it, are perfectly justifiable.

The friends of truth—the patriotic Americans who would sustain their country's honor against foreign rivalry, and defend their country's interests against all assailants, err greatly when they contend with these men on any point but one. Their general principles cannot be refuted; their logic is irresistible; the error, if any there be, is in their premises. They assert that negro slavery is unjust. This, and this al ne, of all they say, is capable of being fairly argued against.

If this proposition cannot be refuted, our Union cannot endure, and it ought not to endure.

Our negro bondmen can neither be exterminated, nor transported to Africa. They are too numerous for either process, and either, if practicable, would involve a violation of humanity. If they were emancipated they would relapse into barbarism, or a set of negro States would arise in our midst, possessing political equality, and entitled to social equality. The division of parties would soon make the negro members a powerful body in Congress—would place some of them in high political stations, and occasionally let one into the Executive chair.

It is in vain to say that this could be endured ; it is simply impossible.

What then remains to be discussed?

The negro race is upon us. With a Constitution which held them in bondage, our Federal Union might be preserved; but if so holding them in bondage be a thing forbidden by God and Nature, we cannot lawfully so hold them, and the Union must perish.

This is the inevitable result of that conflict which has now reached its climax.

Among us, at the north, the sole question for reflection, study, and friendly interchange of thought should be—Is negro slavery unjust? The rational and dispassionate inquirer will find no difficulty in arriving at my conclusion. It is fit and proper; it is, in its own nature, as an institution beneficial to both races ; and the effect of this assertion is not diminished by our admitting that many faults are practised under it. Is not such the fact in respect to all human laws and institutions?

I am, gentlemen, with great respect, yours truly,
CHARLES O'CONOR.

Aside from the occasion, Sagacity, itself, would be in doubt,—whether both, speech, and letter, (more particularly the letter, because more carefully definite)—were intended as a real *defence* of, or keen satire, almost *burlesque*, on the Institution. In the letter, the *anti-slavery argument* is certainly *well put*. Contrarywise—a bold specimen of special pleading, in a bad cause. We contemplate a few remarks upon the *Constitution*, in which place we shall show that this view of slavery is not original ;—but was the cherished picture by South Carolina and Georgia Statesmen, at the time of framing and accepting that *bond* of National Union.

POLITICS ;—POLITICAL ;—POLITY. These terms, by eminence, apply to the organization and administration of Civil Government. They are therefore of *highest* import, as affecting the moral, and material, welfare of a nation. And yet are they so prostituted, *popularly;* like as are the great physical laws of conserving our race; as to prove a moral degeneracy, in their attaching shades of common acceptation and use. Thus *Politics, Political, Politician (Polity,* retaining its proper eminence, because little used, nor generally understood) imply, in common parlance, shrewdness, cunning, intrigue, strategy; and for show of decency, *"conservatism,"* and *"compromise"* : in both postulates, a parallelism, patent to observation. Hence no man of reputation, would feel it a compliment to be designated a *Politician,* even as certain *specialties* in Physical science attach a shade of odium to the professed exclusive operators, "whose trade it is." We advert to this *popular* idea of Politics, mere demagogueism, in order to distinguish the higher, better, proper sense of these terms, and for a special purpose which we proceed briefly to consider.

We repeat, Politics (a concrete term) is, by eminence, the Science of Civil Government. Also,—what we distinctly propounded in our second Lecture,—Civil Government is God's (not man's) *own* Institution for the promotion, and conservation, of man's *moral* and *temporal*— as we now say of the *Church,* of his *spiritual* and *eternal,* welfare. We also opine, on the safer side surely ;— whatever it be, that embraces man's *highest* interests,— virtually includes, by eminent domain, every *subordinate* interest. Politics, then, may not be divorced from Religion, without violence. Hence may be deduced the *duty,* as inseparable from the *privilege,* of the ministers of Religion (nor yet secularizing their peculiar sacred calling) to inculcate, both by *example,* and *precept,* a conscientious discharge of *civil trusts.* In a free Republic, the Ballot-box should ever be had in honor, as the Symbol of *Divinely* delegated Majesty and Power. The Electoral Franchise is Freedom's Gateway to God's own chosen, or permitted, seat of Earthly rule; and should the Enemy come in as a flood, who should hesitate to lift up a standard against him ?

Another view of Politics—illustrating the importance of this science of Government; it is as the science of

Architecture in planning the security, the comforts, conveniences, and the elegancies of our homes. What these are to our families, so is a government to a nation,—the indispensable security of all that is valuable. Fellow Citizens of the United States! as our money and labor are cheerfully invested, without stint, for the *"homes— sweet homes"* of our families; grudge we no needful expenditure for the security of all these,—a *stable Government*, founded upon the Rock of Freedom—(not sands of Slavery) defying the "rains, the floods, and the winds :"—a Habitation meet for a *Christian nation;* needing no resort to the old hats, rugs, or pillows, of "conservatism," and "compromise," to shield the huddling inmates from "the peltings of the pitiless storm."

In this connexion also, we contrast the *practical Atheism* of our day, (perhaps of our *nation*) with our *Theoretical Orthodoxy*, assenting, in all things, to God's supremacy; and yet, in practice, virtually denying all subserviency---even in the matter of *national existence* and *preservation.* In exact point is the following extract---a pearl of "purest ray." We hope to be pardoned for this assumed license; first, in our desire to give the *sentiment* all possible currency, and therefore in style, *most peculiarly fitting;* and second---that our Nutshell shall be secure from condemnation, as *valueless.*

National being is the work of God. A nation is the product of His will, and its continuance the expression of His purpose. Men are not fortuitously aggregated into bodies and communities, as the wanton billows toss the sands into heaps upon the shore. When a nation is to be born, God gives forth the germ, warms it into life, and watches over its growth and development. Away in some secret nook, the rill among the Andes that in time swells to be the Amazon, takes its rise; and as it runs it enlarges, till it comes in time to be a mimic representative of "the multitudinous sea." While God wills a people to be one, it is one; and when He says it shall be one no longer, perhaps in mercy, perhaps in wrath, certainly in equity and in wisdom, it is broken in pieces, it, as it were, falls apart of itself, as the ripened seed-vessel cleaves asunder, and displays an inward and antecedent plurality which had been hidden during its growth. As in its inception and in all its subsequent growth, it obeys a higher will, and follows a law that is exterior to it, so in its dissolution. Yet, there are second causes, numerous, various, potent, all that constitutes the visible phenomena of history, by which its changes are effected. And wise men who look upon them think they find in them the philosophy of history, the principles that regulate the sequence and connection of its events. But there is a higher philosophy, and that is God's will, of which these are the expressions and means, as the chip that floats on the surface is the sign of the current beneath. "The Most High divided to the nations their inheritance : when He separated the sons of Adam, He set the bounds of the people." "He hath made of one blood all the nations of the men, for to dwell on all the face of the earth, and hath determined the times before appointed, and the bounds of their habitation." In God, then. is the nation's being. It is God's creature ; and if it is wise, it will recognize its derivation and its dependence. It will not think that it *is* by man's will or caprice, or *lives* by man's art or strength; above all it will not think of itself so meanly, as to account itself an accident, a promiscuous multitude of men cast together in the fortuitous movements of the ages. That is a very low and mean patriotism that is based upon such opinions. I have no faith in a patriotism that overlooks God. and fails to see in the nation, the outgoing and expression of His Will and His love. "Such wisdom descendeth not from above, but is earthly, sensual, devilish." It can make a pandemonium on earth, such as France once became in the name of patriotism, but it will never yield the fruit of righteousness, or of peace, or of a true and reliable unity. God in the nation, the nation a divine thing, is that which gives the nation a value, that makes its life sacred, and its preservation a thing for which men may wisely peril substance and life, a thing worth making sacrifices for, a thing worth fighting for, yea, worth dying for, if need be, that makes the hero who dies for his country, if he does it intelligently, and on right principles, only second to the martyr who dies for his faith. This renders patriotism a part of every good man's religion, of every true Christian's Christianity. This makes the traitor an offender against Christ ; and rebellion, if there be not some pitiable delusion to excuse it, a renunciation of Christ, and a forfeiture of the Christian character and hope. The saddest spectacle this world can see is the sight of Christian men, yea, of Christian ministers, enrolled under its unholy and God-defying banner, leading its embattled hosts, glorying in its ignominious livery. The great wisdom of the nation, then. is to recognize and honor Christ's headship, to make His law its rule, His power its safeguard, His glory its aim, His service its honor.   *   *   So must every nation do whose unity is more than a sham, whose unity is genuine, steadfast and trustworthy.—*Dr. Hallam, from Sermon on occasion of National Fast, Sept. 26th, 1861.*

DEMOCRACY : REPUBLICANISM : Many pages already prepared, upon these fundamental principles of free Government; and also upon our *"Good old Constitution,"* (see *"song"* at close of 2d Lecture) we are compelled to omit, because exceeding our prescribed limit. Briefly—*Democracy* is *Political Atheism* (in a *Pickwickian* sense) as well expressed in the formula, *"We the People."* It segregates society—separates States.

Both in place, GOOD ; neither, "a BAD, we call ;
Each works its end ; to move, [Dem.] or govern, [Rep.] all."

It is the great *Centrifugal* force, regulated by the *Centripetal* force of *Republicanism*, so happily combined and adjusted, by the Wisdom imparted to our Fathers, in framing our Civil Polity. Really distinct principles are these, yet of strong mutual affinities; and sublimely illustrated in God's universe of worlds; and in the absence of disturbing forces, might well co-operate with Time itself. *Democracy* is dis-social, selfish—*"the spring of action."* *Republicanism* is eminently social, and conservative, converting Democracy to a Commonwealth. The *one*, the raw material; the other, converting to use. *"Vox Populi,"* if of the Heaven-derived *Conscience*, (see first lecture) may be *"Vox Dei;"* but otherwise, most probably *Vox Diaboli*.

And, briefly too, of the *Constitution*. Our form of Government was adjusted, *on trial*, to the genius and condition of the people, wisely providing for further and more complete adjustment, by *amendment*. The Constitution was not a golden calf, to be worshipped. The "Supreme *law*" of the land; *itself* was not declared *Supreme*. *"We the People"* did not thus abdicate the Throne. Its *preamble* is a plain recognition of a "higher law" clearly implying, yea declaring, its own *grand purpose*, and subserviency, as *"Salus populi suprema Lex."* Hence any measures for *this purpose*, dictated by unforeseen exigences of Rebellion and Treason, not inconsistent with Christian civilization, are *eminently* CONSTITUTIONAL; and this too by its own *special* grant of all necessary powers for *complete effect*.

A single further remark on the clause, for the delivery of fugitives "held to service." It is, and was so intended and accepted at the time, *as debates fully prove*, simply a prohibition of Emancipation, in the particular case, by virtue of any law or regulation of another State : giving to the *owner* a clear highway in the race of recovery : at his *own* cost, of course. And, presuming upon mutual comity, in the mere formality of certificate ; the original *fugitive slave law* of 1793, some five years only from the framing of the Constitution, was in exact accordance with this plain, common sense, literal, interpretation, and in exact conformity to the views of the time as expressed in the several State Conventions, accepting the Constitution; wherein there was no disagreement as to *status*, though not agreeing as to its *effect :* some deeming this privilege of recovery, without *impediment* of State law, a reasonable security ; others, little or no security at all. As, in our first Lecture, of the "ten lost verses restored ;" so any engrafted law might well have been incorporated in the Constitution, if in strict accordance therewith, as intended by the Framers themselves, (not by subsequent forced deductions) what then would become of *the* fugitive slave law of modern compromisers? We intended to give some of these debates, but our allotted pages are already filled. (See "*Teachings of Patriots and Statesmen,*" published in Philadelphia, by Bradley, 1860.

OUTLINE HISTORY OF THE INTER-STATE SLAVE TRADE.

We take, for the Outline *History* of the inter-State Slave-trade, a TABLE, (which see for reference in connexion herewith,) ready prepared to our hand from the Census Bureau. Surely, volumes would be required for a tolerable filling of this *Outline*, as sketched in boldest lines in this *Table* of Arabic figures. (It is a trite maxim—"figures cannot lie.") We adopt it as substantially correct for our purpose—not being at the pains to verify it, in every particular, from accidental error, either typographical, or by computation; being satisfied from inspection, and its source—the national archives. Its general view it is, which we assume to be undeniably correct. It speaks volumes on the subject. We find it in the "*Tribune Almanac*, (of much value for reference,) styled—"*Movement of Slave Population.*" We will call it our "Sliding Scale" of differences of actual, and apparent, increase per cent. of slave population in the several Slave States, thus presenting at a glance, a bold outline, Historical, of the inter-State Slave-trade. Now for the Outline ;—[See *Table* on last page.]

Now for example of application of the "Sliding Scale." We find the average increase, per cent, on total sums at

foot of columns, for each decade—ten years—(omitting
first decade, from 1800 ;—the African slave-trade, tolerated until 1808, giving a much larger increase—45.6 per
cent. on sum total ;—and, see Georgia, 102, 9 per cent ;)
from 1810, to be 25.6 per cent ;—(our own computation
of *average, E. E.*) Next we will take Virginia, as having the greatest slave population, where from its gene-
eral advantages of climate, occupation, and more com-
fortable condition, we might expect to find—aided by
speciality process, or system of slave rearing,—even a
much larger than average increase—say 35 to 40 per
cent.,(see increase on *total population* first given,) and
yet she shows an average of 6.6 per cent. only; and
in one decade, 1840 to 1850—an actual decrease of 1.4
per cent. So also of the other border Slave States.
What becomes of the surplus? Why this very small per
centage of increase, in the more favorable border
States,—and vastly greater, in the less favorable, more
southern, and Gulf States? Answer : Inter-state slave-
trade.

Let us now take as a basis of computation, 490,887
the slaves of Virginia, as given in the table for 1860.
At the ratio of 40 per cent. increase, (we think the ratio not too large as before shown) and find the amount
for present decade—now in its 2d year—of numerical
increase 196,354, but at the apparent average increase
since 1810, only 32,395 i. e., 6.6 per cent., showing a
difference of 163,959—doubtless a close approximation to truth ;—and hence, an average *yearly sale* from
Virginia, to other states, of 16,395—an *army !* of men
women and children—or 163,959 in 10 years—suppose
if continued to 1870, as in former decades ! The same
reasoning applies to other border States. Who will
say the *inter-state slave-trade* has not a History ? It
may be *unwritten,*—or but partially, yet boldly, *outlined*
on earth ;—but most accurately and minutely filled in
Heaven !! And this of Virginia !?—the "mother of
Presidents"! where was born, lived and died, a **Washington**! with many noble compeers, and coadjutors in
the race [of Freedom ! Alas! how degenerate.! pros-
titute! sold to infamy ! Is not this same Virginia—

equivocal in policy — assuming, to be umpire;—
neutral, yet menacing—"no coercion of a sister state,
—"Compromise and Conservatism:"—this *pet* of the
nation ; yet pillaging all within her grasp; is not
this same Virginia, the head and front; the heart and
soul ; of this rebellion ? And what is her present sit-.
uation ? laid waste by hostile armies; sundered and
shaken as by earthquake! How suited are God's judg-
ments! Her map is but a picture of retributions.

In corroboration of our position, hear one of her
earlier noble sons, Thos. J. Randolph, in the Va. Leg-
islature of 1832. Extract from debates :

"It is a practice, and an increasing practice, in parts of Virginia, to
rear slaves for market. How can an honorable mind, a patriot and a
lover of his country, bear to see this Ancient Dominion, rendered illustrious by the noble devotion and patriotism of her sons in the cause
of liberty, converted into one grand menagerie, where men are to be
reared for the market, like oxen for the shambles? Is it better, is it
not worse, than the slave trade—that trade which enlisted the labor
of the good and wise of every creed, and every clime, to abolish it?
The trader receives the slave, a stranger in language, aspect, and manners, from the merchant who has brought him from the interior. The
ties of father, mother, husband, and child, have all been rent in twain;
before he receives him his soul has become callous. But here, sir, in-
dividuals whom the master has known, from infancy, whom he has
seen sporting in the innocent gambols of childhood, who have been
accustomed to look to him for protection, he tears from a mothers'
arms, and sells into a strange country, among strange people, subject
to cruel taskmasters.

"He has attempted to justify slavery here, because it exists in Africa, and has stated that it exists all over the world. Upon the same
principle he could justify Mahometanism, with its plurality of wives,
petty wars of plunder, robbery and murder, or any other of the abominations and enormities of savage tribes. Does slavery exist in any
part of civilized Europe ? No, sir, in no part of it."

Here is the *shading* of the historic page of the inter-
state slave trade. Yes, verily, Virginia! the Old Dominion ; the boast of chivalry; openly, boldly declares
her *sympathy* with the slave rebellion, for the *evident*
principal reason, that she constitutes herself, by her
cherished policy, the *cis-Atlantic Africa*, of slave
supply! of slave trade!! Her position, her history,
her influence, and her arrogance, constitute her the

responsible leader of the rebellion, first, by covert countenance, and last by open embraces; giving her *Capitol* to the reign of slavery; illustrating her characteristic lust of "Dominion"; appropos, of the fitting adage, "Better reign in H--l, than serve in Heaven."

And yet another glance at our sliding scale: we see the slaves of Virginia in 1800, numbered 345,796; double and treble, of other principal slave states, and 7-17ths, or nearly one-half the entire slave population of the nation. Again we see the *total* of slaves in 1860, more than 4 1-2 times greater than in 1800—a ratio of increase doubtless fully equal to, or exceeding, that of the entire *native* population of the nation, aside from the vast and constant immigration from other countries: and yet the increase in Virginia, for the entire period of sixty years, is little more than 1-4th, instead of 4 1-2 times. Is not this *incontestible proof that Virginia, prima inter pares!* is the *foster-mother* of Slavery in the United States!--Queen of courtezans--the Cleopatra at the National Capital, debauching the very *elect*—reducing the *Government* to subservience! the very Procuress, Mistress, Beldam of the brothel!— We say then, as to a pupil in music, *"study the scales."* *"What need we of any further witnesses?"*

If it be charged we have employed a figure inappropriate for " ears polite," as of things " not to be named as becometh saints,"---we only answer, we are not now speaking of *"Saints."* The suggestion in our mind finds warrant in the striking correspondence with the *scarlet* —— of the Apocalyptic vision, (Rev. xvii and xviii,) especially, and literally, in the items, *"slaves, and souls of men"*---say twelve to fifteen thousand sold annually! or nearly one million within the last sixty years! and is this correspondence to be traced still farther? to the end of the chapter? *"And in her was found the blood of prophets and of saints, and of all that were slain upon the Earth?"*

Of *The African Slave trade;* we had designed to give an outline of some pages, drawn principally from the *Edinburgh Encyclopedia;* but our prescribed space affords not room even for the briefest abstract. We barely note as follows, to wit: "This trade was first begun by the Portuguese about the year 1481. The manner of first obtaining, and next of transporting slaves, styled the *"middle passage,"* in which "the best ships afforded scarcely as much room for a slave, as a man has in his coffin,"---so that "about one-fourth die on the passage;" and nearly as many more during the first ten years---or period of seasoning."---the annual loss thus resulting, computed at 45,000, was indeed shocking to humanity! Measures for the abolition of the trade were initiated about the year 1787. Sharpe, Clarkson, and Wilberforce, aided by others like-minded, were the leading spirits; but for full twenty years their persevering efforts were continually baffled, until the measure was at last triumphantly carried in Parliament, in 1807 ; 283 to 16.

The abolition of Slavery itself, under British rule, is the well-known glorious record of our own day.

The *Radicals---Fanatics;* Clarksons, Wilberforces, Sumners, Lovejoys, Phillipses; Gerritt Smiths; &c, &c , a word here as to these. Sturdy, staunch, *super-erect*---i. e. inclining more or less to an opposite extreme--Cosmopolitanism---and *alleged* "negro equality"--&c., seemingly essaying to "make straight what God has made crooked." yet, indispensable withal--according to a well-known law of *mechanics,* as *moral purchase pillars,* for elevating the *prone* and *crouching* to an *upright* position. Heaven has its adaptations in exact, overmatching, counter-plot to slavery, and H--l. When did ever the ALMIGHTY dispense with his *Elijahs* for "troubling" a wicked nation ?

On the Subjects---*Democracy,* and *Republicanism,* we would have demonstrated more fully, and clearly, the importance of a just *equilibrium* of these elements, both in civil, and ecclesiastical polity. Also, on the *Constitution*; its purity, as regards *Slavery.* We know too, Pertinacity will still cling to its hobby; and of others, the •hope is vain of overcoming peculiar mental *idio*(syncra)*cy.* "We speak as to WISE MEN."

ERRATA. Without particular reference, we discover occasional slight typographical errors in our *Nutshell,* for future correction.

www.ingramcontent.com/pod-product-compliance
Lightning Source LLC
Chambersburg PA
CBHW020253090426
42735CB00010B/1901

Michael Ferrebee Sadler

The sacrament of responsibility
Testimony of Scripture to the teaching of the church on holy baptism

ISBN/EAN: 9783337282820

Printed in Europe, USA, Canada, Australia, Japan

Cover: Foto ©Lupo / pixelio.de

More available books at **www.hansebooks.com**

THE

Sacrament of Responsibility;

OR

TESTIMONY OF SCRIPTURE

TO THE

TEACHING OF THE CHURCH

ON

Holy Baptism,

WITH ESPECIAL REFERENCE TO THE CASE OF INFANTS,
AND ANSWERS TO OBJECTIONS.

BY THE REV. M. F. SADLER, M.A.
Vicar of Bridgwater.

Sixth Edition.

LONDON:

PUBLISHED AND SOLD BY BELL & DALDY, 186, FLEET STREET;
AND J. HALL & SON, CAMBRIDGE.
1861.

ADVERTISEMENT.

THE following pages were written to supply a want, felt by the writer as a Parish Minister, of a short treatise in which the doctrine of the Church on Baptism, and her application of that doctrine to the case of all Baptized Infants, should be proved from Scripture alone; and the objections commonly urged against it, fully and fairly stated, and answered on principles which the objectors themselves acknowledge. The writer has endeavoured to shew, that *every Scripture reason for the practice of Infant baptism, is equally a reason for believing that God blesses all Infants, in that Sacrament, with the grace He has annexed to the outward sign.*

He has entitled the Tract, "The Sacrament of Responsibility," because he finds that the Apostles (and especially St Paul), hold all the Baptized responsible for grace received at their Baptism, as will be abundantly manifest from an attentive perusal of *Romans* vi.; 1 *Corinthians* vi. x. xii.; *Colossians* ii. iii. He would refer the reader who desires to pursue further the line of Scripture argument entered upon in this Tract, to his subsequent work "The Second Adam and the New Birth." (Bell and Daldy.) May God be pleased to bless this Tract to the edification of His Church for Jesus Christ's sake.